# THE 100+ SERIES™

# READING COMPREHENSION

**Essential Practice for Advanced Reading Comprehension Topics**

**Grade 8**

Carson-Dellosa Publishing LLC
Greensboro, North Carolina

**Credits**
Content Editor: Nancy Rogers Bosse
Proofreader: Carrie D'Ascoli

Visit *carsondellosa.com* for correlations to Common Core, state, national, and Canadian provincial standards.

Carson-Dellosa Publishing LLC
PO Box 35665
Greensboro, NC 27425 USA
carsondellosa.com

ISBN 978-1-4838-1578-7
03-134187784

# Table of Contents

# Introduction

Organized by specific reading skills, this book is designed to enhance students' reading comprehension. The engaging topics provide meaningful and focused practice. The reading passages are presented in a variety of genres, including fiction, nonfiction, and poetry. Subject matter from across the curriculum, including topics from science, history, and literary classics, deepens student knowledge while strengthening reading skills.

The grade-appropriate selections in this series are an asset to any reading program. Various reading skills and concepts are reinforced throughout the book through activities that align to the Common Core State Standards in English language arts. To view these standards, please see the Common Core Alignment Chart on page 4.

# Common Core Alignment Chart

| Common Core State Standards* | | Practice Page(s) |
|---|---|---|
| **Reading Standards for Literature** | | |
| Key Ideas and Details | 8.RL.1–8.RL.3 | 20–23, 36–43, 46, 47, 56–60, 62–65, 68–77, 83–93, 106–119 |
| Craft and Structure | 8.RL.4–8.RL.6 | 36, 37, 62–65, 94–99, 102–111 |
| Integration of Knowledge and Ideas | 8.RL.7–8.RL.9 | 86, 87, 112–119 |
| Range of Reading and Level of Text Complexity | 8.RL.10 | 20–23, 36–43, 46, 47, 56–60, 62–65, 68–77, 83–99, 102–119 |
| **Reading Standards for Informational Text** | | |
| Key Ideas and Details | 8.RI.1–8.RI.3 | 5–19, 24–35, 44, 45, 48–55, 61, 66–67, 78–84, 100–101, 120, 121 |
| Craft and Structure | 8.RI.4–8.RI.6 | 5–19, 24–27, 50, 51, 54, 55, 61, 66, 67, 78–81, 100, 101, 120, 121 |
| Integration of Knowledge and Ideas | 8.RI.7–8.RI.9 | 54, 55, 66, 67, 120, 121 |
| Range of Reading and Level of Text Complexity | 8.RI.10 | 5–19, 24–35, 44, 45, 48–55, 61, 66, 67, 78–81, 100, 101, 120, 121 |
| **Writing Standards** | | |
| Text Types and Purposes | 8.W.1–8.W.3 | 10, 11, 24–27, 34, 35, 38, 39, 42, 43, 47–49, 52, 53, 60, 61, 76–85, 100, 101, 107, 112–119 |
| Production and Distribution of Writing | 8.W.4–8.W.6 | 10, 11, 16, 17 |
| Research to Build and Present Knowledge | 8.W.7–8.W.9 | 6, 7, 80, 81 |
| Range of Writing | 8.W.10 | 6, 7, 10, 11, 16, 17, 24–27, 34, 35, 38, 39, 42, 43, 47–49, 52, 53, 60, 61, 76–85, 100, 101, 107, 112–119 |
| **Language Standards** | | |
| Knowledge of Language | 8.L.3 | 32, 33, 36–39, 68, 69, 78, 79 |
| Vocabulary Acquisition and Use | 8.L.4–8.L.6 | 36, 37, 54, 55, 94–105 |

* © Copyright 2010. National Governors Association Center for Best Practices and Council of Chief State School Officers. All rights reserved.

Read the passage. Then, answer the questions. Cite evidence from the text to support your responses.

# Birds of a Feather

A bird spreads its wings as it stands upon the top of an anthill. Is it playing king of the mountain? Probably not. Ants secrete a substance that acts like an antibiotic. The bird may be seeking the medicinal substance to rub over its feathers to kill parasites. Birds have also been seen rubbing crushed ants through their feathers or smearing themselves with the juice from onions or limes if ants are not available.

Dale Clayton, a biologist with the University of Utah, calls this strange behavior a life-or-death activity. Feather lice can destroy a bird's insulating feathers, forcing the bird to use enormous amounts of energy just to keep warm. Without the medicinal substance a bird's weight can drop which can cause death. When some male birds are infected with mites, their tails do not grow as long as other male. Shorter tails mean fewer mates.

Have you ever seen a bird busily grooming itself? You may think this behavior is for vanity reasons, but actually this strange behavior is another life-or-death activity. Some zoologists have noted that a clean male bird is an attractive male. That may explain why a male horned guan, a Central American bird somewhat like a turkey, takes dust baths whenever he spots a female he would like to mate with.

The next time you see birds grooming, look again. You may be witnessing a life-or-death struggle.

1.  What is the main idea of this passage?

    _____

    _____

    _____

2.  List three facts that support the main idea.

    _____

    _____

    _____

    _____

Read the passage. Then, answer the questions on page 7.

# Life in Yakutia

Many people who live in colder climates look forward to spring. Even if we embrace winter with all of its seasonal pleasures—skiing, ice hockey, and skating—we look forward to the day in March when the snow starts to disappear. So imagine a place that is so cold that a temperature just above freezing is considered a warm day. Imagine living in a place where your breath actually turns to ice the moment you step outside.

A place like this exists in a region of Russia called Yakutia. Located in the eastern part of Russia known as Siberia, it is one of the coldest areas in the world. In the town of Yakutsk, inhabitants have stated that it gets so cold that a corridor forms in the shape of a silhouette when a person walks down the street. The person's body heat actually cuts a path through the icy air, a path that others can see. After a person has passed out of sight, the corridor remains, hanging in the bright, cold air.

Some parts of Siberia receive between 30 and 50 inches (76–127 cm) of snow each year. But Yakutia has very little precipitation. You might think this is a good thing, but as a result, the region lacks the natural insulation that snow provides. The Yakutians layer the snow that does fall over their houses to form icy coatings to retain the heat. A traditional Yakutian house is a one-story, rectangular cabin with a nearly flat roof. Made of logs, it is sealed with mud, which also acts as insulation against the bitter cold.

Everything in Yakutia is built on permafrost. **Permafrost** is ground made up of ice and soil that stays frozen for most of the year. In fact, half of the landmass of Russia rests on permafrost. Permafrost causes problems because it has an active layer that freezes in the winter and thaws during the summer. The thickness of this layer ranges from 3 to 10 feet (0.9–3 m). With the ground shifting so dramatically, it makes the construction of roads, buildings, pipelines, and other structures difficult. It's even difficult to dig graves in permafrost because of the instability of the ground. The Yakutians bury their dead in above-ground structures instead.

You might think that spring and summer would give the people of Yakutia a special sense of relief, but you would be wrong. Spring spells disaster for the inhabitants of this region. When the temperatures rise, their houses sink as the permafrost gives way. Sometimes only the roofs of houses can be seen from the street. Temperatures above freezing mean chaos in Yakutia. Mud oozes everywhere and tiny rivers of melted snow flood towns and settlements.

When winter returns, stability returns with it. The sub-zero temperatures put everything back in order. Houses, roads, and the ground itself stay glued together like the pieces of a model-train village. Paths and roads become passable again. In winter, life returns to normal.

Use the passage on page 6 to answer the questions.

1.  What is the main idea of this passage?

    A.  Houses sometimes disappear in Yakutia.

    B.  The people of Yakutia face special challenges because of the weather.

    C.  Yakutia is located in Siberia, in eastern Russia.

    D.  Spring is not the favorite season in Yakutia.

2.  Which of these is a supporting detail from the passage?

    A.  Spring is a favorite time of year for many people because of the warmer weather.

    B.  Life returns to normal at different times of the year in different places.

    C.  The active layer of permafrost causes houses and roads in Yakutia to sink in the spring.

    D.  The towns in Yakutia are like model-train villages.

3.  Which of these is not a supporting detail from the passage?

    A.  The weather in Yakutia is bitterly cold with many snowstorms.

    B.  Yakutian houses are built with logs and sealed with mud to make them warm.

    C.  It is so cold in Yakutia that a person's breath can freeze as soon as he steps outside.

    D.  People in Yakutia use the snow that does fall to layer over their homes.

4.  How does the author use comparisons to make the point that the weather in Yakutia presents challenges? Look for comparison words like *you might think . . . but.*

    _____

    _____

5.  Would you like to live in Yakutia? Why or why not? Cite evidence from the text.

    _____

    _____

Read the passage. Then, complete the graphic organizer on page 9.

# The Indigo Highway

(1) Most people don't think of turtles as fast swimmers. How, then, do slow and clumsy loggerhead turtles wind up in Nova Scotia—thousands of miles from their Caribbean home? It isn't persistence that brings these turtles north. It's the Gulf Stream, a current that originates in the water south of Florida and ends up off the Grand Banks of Newfoundland, where it joins the North Atlantic current. The loggerhead turtles, along with giant blue fin tuna, blue sharks, and swordfish, hitch rides on this current, which moves faster than the ocean water around it.

(2) The Gulf Stream is like a giant river flowing within the ocean. It is between 50 and 100 miles wide (80.5 km–161 km) and about one mile (1.6 km) deep. It moves much more water than any river on Earth—150 million cubic meters of water per second. That's 100 times the flow of all of the rivers in the world combined. It's not really possible to see the flow of this stream, but you can recognize it by its indigo, or deep blue, color. The Gulf Stream is also warmer than the northern Atlantic waters to its left and cooler than the Sargasso Sea to its right. In many ways, it acts as a barrier between these two sections of the Atlantic, deflecting the warmer water toward Europe.

(3) The Gulf Stream made its mark on history by affecting European travel to and from the New World. In 1519, Ponce de Léon's ship pilot, Antonio de Alaminos, discovered that sailing with the stream back to Europe saved a tremendous amount of time. This route became known as the "Highway of the Indies." Early sea captains who learned of it kept the directions a secret from competing traders. A century later, the Pilgrims had a very different experience with the Gulf Stream. It appears that they sailed against it, which is why their sea voyage took a lengthy 66 days. It may also explain how they ended up in Massachusetts instead of their original destination, Virginia. If they had crossed the Gulf Stream, it would have launched them north to New England.

(4) Benjamin Franklin showed a little more savvy when it came to understanding the ways of the Gulf Stream. While working in London just before the Revolutionary War, complaints reached him about the slowness of mail delivery from Great Britain to the colonies. He asked his cousin, a Nantucket whaling-ship captain, about this. His cousin told him that he and other whaling crews had seen British mail ships making slow progress while sailing in the Gulf Stream's current. The whaling ships, in contrast, used the stream to chase whales and make their capture possible. When the whaling ships tried to offer friendly advice to the mail ships, the British rejected the information and said they were "too wise to be counseled by simple American fishermen." Franklin continued to study the stream. Along with his cousin, he devised three amazingly accurate maps charting its course. Later, during his own voyages across the Atlantic, he followed the Gulf Stream's path by recording its warmer water temperatures with a thermometer.

(5) Oceanographers, amateur students of the sea, and others continue to take an interest in the Gulf Stream. Many features of this huge current remain a fascinating mystery. In the meantime, loggerhead turtles and other sea creatures happily take their free rides on the indigo highway of the ocean.

Use the passage on page 8 to complete the graphic organizer to analyze the organization of the passage. Cite evidence from the text to support your responses.

| Main Idea of the Article | | |
| --- | --- | --- |
| **Paragraph 1: Introduction** | | |
| **Paragraph 2** | **Paragraph 3** | **Paragraph 4** |
| Main Idea | Main Idea | Main Idea |
| Detail | Detail | Detail |
| Detail | Detail | Detail |
| Detail | Detail | Detail |
| Detail | Detail | Detail |
| **Paragraph 5: Conclusion** | | |

Read the passage. Then, answer the questions on page 11.

# Dog Data

Do you consider a dog your best friend? Many people do. Even if you don't it might be interesting to learn some facts about this species that has lived with humans for thousands of years. Some scientists who study animal behavior believe that dogs could be descended from wolves. Another theory is that dogs are the animal cousins of wolves, with dogs and wolves sharing a common ancestor. For this reason, the study of wolf behavior has proven to be helpful in understanding the actions of dogs.

**Why Do Dogs Bury Bones?**

A look at the behavior of wolves tells us something about how canines handle food. Single wolves and small groups of wolves can eat some of their prey in one sitting—animals ranging in size from rabbits to sheep. In fact, one adult wolf can eat the equivalent of 176 quarter-pound hamburgers in a day! That might be where the expression "wolf down one's food" comes from. However, large prey such as cattle or caribou can be more meat than a small pack of wolves can consume. Rather than leave the surplus for vultures, the thrifty wolves bury their leftovers and dig them up the next day for another meal. Dogs follow this behavior when they bury bones. Even though a dog is fed every day, its instinct tells it to treat the bone as surplus food to be saved and savored again.

**Why Do Dogs Bark?**

Let's look to wolves again. Wolves bark to warn the members of the pack of a possible threat. A wolf's bark prompts the adults in the pack to hide their pups and prepare for action. The bark of a wolf is terse and relatively quiet. By contrast, a dog's bark can be noisy and prolonged. But the purpose of the barking is the same. Dogs' barks are warnings to their human family. The dog is saying, "I notice something unusual. Pay attention!" A barking dog is not necessarily getting ready to attack. The barking is simply telling others to be alert.

**Why Does My Dog Want to Sleep in My Bed?**

Almost every dog views its human owners as members of its pack. It considers the house in which it lives to be its den. Dogs, like wolves, are protective of their pack members and prefer to huddle together for security. That's why dogs like to sleep with their owners. Sharing a bed with a dog may be against the rules in some homes, but keeping the dog in the basement or in a kennel isn't wise either. In the wild, only outcast wolves sleep away from the pack, usually because they have been driven away. A dog that is forced to sleep in isolation will start to feel and act like an outcast. Human owners who find a way to let their dogs sleep as near to them as possible often have fewer problems with their pets.

Years of breeding and living in the world of humans have made dogs some of the best animal friends we have.

Use the passage on page 10 to answer the questions.

1. Scientists believe that dogs and wolves

    A. have nothing in common.

    B. could be animal cousins.

    C. may share a common ancestor.

    D. both B and C

2. What kind of scientific research on wolves has been a help in understanding the actions of dogs?

    A. life expectancy

    B. hunting habits

    C. behavior

    D. both A and B

3. For what reason do wolves bury leftover food?

    A. to save it for the next day

    B. to hide it from scavengers

    C. to fertilize the soil

    D. both A and B

4. The sound of a barking wolf is

    A. quiet.

    B. loud.

    C. terse.

    D. both A and C

5. How do dogs view their human owners?

    A. as pack members

    B. as enemies

    C. as outcasts

    D. both B and C

6. Why do some wolves sleep away from the pack?

    A. they don't like the pack

    B. they are outcasts

    C. the den is too crowded

    D. both B and C

7. How does the author organize the information in this article?

    _____

8. How does the author feel about dogs? Cite evidence from the text to support your response.

    _____

    _____

    _____

Read the passage. Then, answer the questions on page 13.

# The Life of Mozart—Triumph or Tragedy?

Can you imagine a five-year-old **composing** and playing music on a child-sized violin? This was true of Mozart, a young genius who grew up to be one of the most creative composers of all time. Do you ever envy people you perceive as having more talent than yourself? From this introduction, you might assume that the life of this gifted child was charmed. Read on. Decide for yourself.

Wolfgang Amadeus Mozart was born in January of 1756 into a musical family. His father, Leopold was a composer and musician and his older sister Anna Maria played the piano. Leopold recognized the giftedness of his children and devoted himself to their careers. Mozart and his sister toured the royal courts of Europe, playing concerts for the nobility. Both of the Mozart children were **prodigies**, but Wolfgang was remarkable. He could listen to any piece of music once and then play it from memory. He could play the **keyboard** or the violin blindfolded. Music that Mozart wrote at the age of five was as good as works by many adult composers.

When Mozart was a young man, he fell in love with a German singer named Aloysia Weber. His parents didn't approve of this relationship and the relationship ended poorly. Later, Mozart fell in love and married Aloysia's younger sister Constanze. Although his family did not approve of this marriage, the young couple enjoyed their life together.

Mozart earned a living selling his **compositions**, giving **concerts**, and providing music lessons to the wealthy. Some of the **operas** Mozart wrote such as *The Marriage of Figaro*, *The Magic Flute*, and *Don Giovanni*, are still performed today. Mozart also wrote music for the court of the Emperor of Austria. He composed 41 **symphonies**. However, none of these ventures earned him much money, and he spent far more than he was able to earn. Mozart often waited until the last moment to work on pieces that had been **commissioned**, or paid for in advance. He wrote the **overture** to *Don Giovanni* the night before it was to be performed.

By the spring of 1791, Mozart was ill and depressed. He was deeply in debt. His health, which had never been good, was declining. A stranger asked Mozart to write a requiem, a musical piece for a funeral. Mozart agreed, but then began to fear that the requiem was being written for his own death. His fears were justified. Mozart died in December of 1791, at the age of 35.

Use the passage on page 12 to answer the questions. Cite evidence from the text to support your responses.

1. What is the main idea of this passage?

   _____

   _____

2. List three details that support the view that Mozart's life was triumphant and three details that support the view that his life was tragic.

| Triumphant | Tragic |
|---|---|
|  |  |

3. Do you feel the life of Mozart was triumphant or tragic?

   _____

   _____

   _____

4. The article includes music-specific words. Define each word using context clues or a dictionary if needed.

   compose: _____

   prodigy: _____

   keyboard: _____

   concert: _____

   composition: _____

   opera: _____

   symphony: _____

   commission: _____

   overture: _____

Read the passage. Then, complete the activity on page 15.

# Extra! Extra! Read All About It!

Whether you get your news from reading a newspaper or a news website, both sources of information are divided into sections. When looking for specific news or information, it helps to understand what kind of information you can find in each section.

The *Front Page* contains the most important news of the day. This news might be local or world news or it may cover business, sports, weather, or arts and entertainment. News websites are able to update this information as it occurs, whereas newspapers can only update it prior to printing—usually once a day. The *World News* section contains news about world events. The *National News* section contains news pertaining to the nation. The *Local* or *Metro News* section contains news about local events. Sometimes local news will become world news when the information affects people outside the locality of the news. For example, wildfires in a particular area may become world news or a kidnapping of a celebrity may become world news. The *Weather* section will include the daily weather and any news about weather-related events. The *Business* or *Financial* section contains articles about the business world. Readers can learn about new companies or changes in companies. They can also read about daily changes in the stock market. The *Sports* section includes news about sports. It will include sports scores and results. This section may cover local, national, and world sports news. The *Arts and Entertainment* or *Leisure* section, like the sports section, may cover local, national, and world arts and entertainment news. This section includes information about celebrities, theater, television, movies, music, dance, literature, and more. The *Opinion* or *Editorial* section contains opinions of people about a variety of subjects. In this section, the objective style of reporting is replaced with the writer's opinion on a news topic or event. Often this section includes regular contributors and a section for readers to write in to express their opinions. The *Obituaries* section gives information on deaths. The *Classified* section includes advertisements of all kinds. Newspapers and news websites may also include a variety of other sections such as *Food, Humor,* or *Travel.* The inclusion of these sections depends on the readers the newspaper or news website is trying to attract.

Read the information about the sections of a newspaper or news website on page 14. Then, match each headline with the section in which you would expect to find the corresponding information.

**Newspaper Sections**

A. Front Page
B. World News
C. National News
D. Local or Metro News

E. Weather
F. Business or Financial
G. Sports

H. Arts and Entertainment or Leisure
I. Opinion or Editorial
J. Classified

_____ 1. New York Metropolitan Opera Opens Tonight

_____ 2. Major Earthquake Rocks Tokyo

_____ 3. The Toronto Maple Leafs Clinch Title

_____ 4. More Rain Expected

_____ 5. Washington High School Band Performs in the Rose Bowl

_____ 6. For Sale: Upright Piano. Excellent Condition. Make Offer.

_____ 7. Could an Outbreak of Swine Flu Spread to North America?

_____ 8. Robbery at Local Shopping Mall

_____ 9. Running Shoe Company Introduces a New Line

_____ 10. Star's Latest Movie is a Box Office Hit

_____ 11. Monet Exhibit Opens in London

_____ 12. Super Bowl Commercials Gross More Than Ever

_____ 13. President to Deliver the State of the Union Address

_____ 14. Hurricane Julia to Hit the East Coast

_____ 15. Light Electronics to Buy New Company

Read the news article. Then, complete the activities on page 17.

# Local Students Display Art in Paris

Three students from the Frank Lloyd Wright School of the Performing Arts represented their school in the International Exhibit of Student Art in Paris, France from June 17–21. The students and their teacher Mr. Kaminski flew to Paris to attend the exhibit. All three students entered sculptures.

Jorge Lopez, a seventh grader, created an enormous papier mâché structure he calls *The Golden Gargoyle*. Its massive head, of rocklike nature and stoic form, peers down as though scrutinizing the mere mortals standing below. This creature is fitted with comic, playful wings much too small to lift his bulky form. The beast appears to wear a long tunic of metal disks, scale-like, almost reptilian, which cover him from shoulder to knee. His feet, oddly enough, are webbed like a platypus.

Chandra Dumon, an eighth grader, chose clay as her medium to mold an exquisite form called *The Supper Table*. Dumon's clay form rests on a low, square, thick-legged table textured with a heavy oak-grain surface. Upon this table rest two simple mugs and plates glazed a deep royal blue. Beside each plate is set a knife and fork so silver-like it fools even the most careful viewer. Clay-form breads, cheeses, and various fruits glazed in realistic color are spread upon the table. Finally, placed at the table's center is a rustic, wood-like candlestick holding the only real object, a white wax candle.

The third entry is a marvelous paper creation by Christopher Mori called *Metropolis 2500*. It is a futuristic cityscape of rounded towers, pointed spires, octahedral and dodecahedral structures, spheres, and prisms of various dimensions. Visually, the form pulls together with ribbon-like highways which swoop and soar through the city plan. Futuristic vehicles for air and land are strategically placed to pique the viewer's interest. Mori is a senior this year and plans on continuing his art education at a university in Paris.

Use the article on page 16 to complete the activities.

1.  Complete the chart using the 5 **W**s to gather information from the news article.

| **W**ho? | |
|----------|---|
| **W**hat? | |
| **W**hen? | |
| **W**here? | |
| **W**hy? | |

2.  Write three questions you have about the people or event mentioned in the article that were not answered in the article?

_____

_____

_____

3.  Although this news article is fictional, where could you find the answers to your questions in question 2 if the people and event were real?

_____

4.  Use your imagination to answer the questions in question 2. Stay with the style and tone of the article.

_____

_____

_____

_____

_____

Read the passage. Then, complete the outline on page 19.

# Northern Lights

For thousands of years, people have seen multicolored rays of light streaking upward in the sky. Many Native American tribes thought that the lights were an omen, a sign of something to come. Some tribes thought that the lights were an omen of war. Others believed that they were human spirits carrying torches to the sky. The Inuit people believed that the lights were the spirits of seals, caribou, and whales.

Europeans reacted to these lights, too. In AD 37, a group of people living outside of Ostia, Italy, thought that the colony was on fire. Rushing to the horizon, they found no fire just the fiery lights in the sky. In 1583, people in France who saw the lights flocked to churches to pray. They thought that the lights were an omen of the end of the world.

These mysterious lights are now known as aurora borealis or the northern lights. They are solar-powered. The sun emits charged particles in all directions. A cloud of these particles is called plasma. The stream of plasma coming from the sun is called the solar wind. When the solar wind disturbs the Earth's magnetic field, the particles glow and create the aurora borealis.

These lights, although beautiful, can create a lot of problems because of the great amount of energy they use. One display can use as much energy as is used by the entire population of the United States in a day! The charged particles bounce around the planet's magnetic field and cause atmospheric disturbance that affects a number of objects. Compasses point the wrong way, communications systems can be disrupted, and power systems can go out. Satellite computers can malfunction. Once, taxi drivers in Alaska received radio dispatches from a cab company in New Jersey. You can imagine the confusion that caused!

The aurora borealis sometimes lights up the sky with bands of pink, red, green, and blue rays of light. At other times, they are colorless but look like long curtains waving across the sky. Newscasters and weather people usually report when the northern lights are performing. Try to catch this information so you won't miss the show.

Use the passage on page 18 to complete the outline.

**I.  Many People Have Seen the Lights**

    A.  Native Americans

        1.  _____

        2.  _____

        3.  Intuits thought they were spirits of light

    B.  _____

        1.  thought colony was on fire

        2.  _____

**II.  Mysterious Lights**

    A.  aurora borealis

        1.  _____

        2.  emit charged particles

            a.  plasma

**III.  Problems**

    A.  Use a lot of energy

    B.  _____

        1.  compasses point wrong direction

        2.  _____

        3.  power systems go out

        4.  _____

**IV.  Beauty of Aurora Borealis**

    A.  _____

    B.  _____

Read the passage. Then, complete the activity on page 21.

# New Kid on the Block

Carter just moved into a new neighborhood. It's not easy to move when you're in middle school. Carter already had a good group of friends in his old neighborhood, but nobody asked him when it was time to move. His dad's job transferred their family. There wasn't much he could do. The realtor who helped his parents purchase their new home assured Carter his new neighborhood was not only walking distance from his new school, but had lots of kids his age.

The first day in his new neighborhood, Carter was overwhelmed at the greetings from the neighborhood kids. It seemed kids poured out of the woodwork just to meet the new kid on the block. Carter met kids who were in elementary school, kids who were in high school, and four kids in particular who were his age and had similar interests to his. The only problem was he met so many kids that first day that he had trouble remembering who was who and what they liked to do. He did remember that the four middle school kids were named Derek, Luke, Lily, and Gabe. He also remembered their last names were Chu, Katz, Lee, and Park but couldn't remember which last name went with which first name. He knew they all lived on his street and they lived at 116, 118, 125, and 132, but he couldn't remember who lived where. One of the kids liked skateboarding, another like doing bike tricks, another played street hockey, and the other played lacrosse in the field in back of the school. Carter liked all those activities and did them with friends in his old neighborhood.

Later that night, Carter sat down and made a chart like the one on page 21. He made notes of the information he could remember. Then he pieced the information together and figured out who was who, where they lived, and what they liked to do.

Read the information that Carter could remember from his conversations with the four middle school kids on page 20. Fill in the graph to determine where each middle school kid lives, what their last name is, and what activity they like to participate in.

The girl's first and last name and the activity all started with the same letter and she lived next door to Gabe.

Derek lived across the street from the rest of the kids. He had set up a net between his house and the house at 127.

The children in the Chu family all had names that started with the letter D.

Gabe Park lives at 118. He was wearing a helmet and carrying a tire pump when Carter met him.

|       | Chu | Park | Lee | Katz | 116 | 118 | 125 | 132 | SB | B | H | L |
|-------|-----|------|-----|------|-----|-----|-----|-----|----|----|----|----|
| Derek |     |      |     |      |     |     |     |     |    |   |   |   |
| Luke  |     |      |     |      |     |     |     |     |    |   |   |   |
| Lily  |     |      |     |      |     |     |     |     |    |   |   |   |
| Gabe  |     |      |     |      |     |     |     |     |    |   |   |   |

Read the passage. Then, complete the activity.

# Class Schedules

Mandy was excited when she got her new class schedule. She texted nine of her closest friends to see who she had classes with. Below are their responses. Her schedule rocked. She had at least one class with each of her friends. This year was sure to be the best! Read Mandy's text and complete the Venn diagram to show which of her friends have which classes with her.

Rachel says:
I have English, band, and math with you!

Nadia says:
We have math and band together!

Lee says:
Band is gonna be a blast!

Nicole says:
I have English Honors, too. Yikes!

Jaime says:
I have band and math with you!

Hannah says:
U, R, N, and I in English! OMG!

Ian says:
Bummer we don't have math together, but band will be fun!

Ryan says:
Go, Knights! Our band's the best!

Mario says:
See U in math!

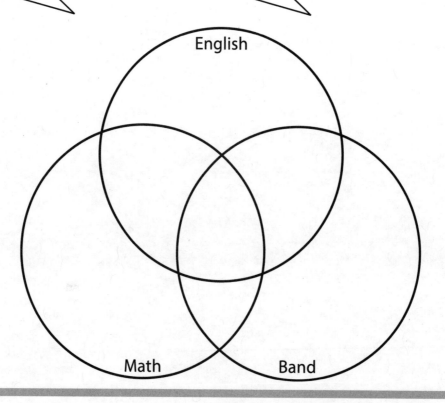

Choose a title that best summarizes each paragraph. Write the title on the line. Use a dictionary if needed.

# Let's Sum It Up

Instincts Save a Life
A Serendipitous Find

A Mythical Visitor
Shock at Lack of Respect

1. _____

It was one of the coldest days in New York City when Becky bought the newspaper at the kiosk. Becky worked for a magazine publisher; she was a writer for the human interest section of the magazine. She purchased the paper every morning scouring it for ideas to include in her magazine. This morning out of the corner of her eye, Becky noticed a young boy fidgeting outside the store next to the kiosk. Becky had a sense that this boy's story would be more interesting than any story in today's paper.

2. _____

With a grateful heart, the beast entered the stable offered by the kind man. Her instincts told her she could trust this two-legged creature. The stable hand, too, was grateful, for he knew he had encountered a rare find. He shook his head and clucked his tongue, "To think that I should be visited by such a majestic beast as the mythical unicorn."

3. _____

He woke from his slumber, coughing. The young urchin looked around the abandoned building where he sought refuge. It looked the same, but the smell of smoke was undeniable. He knew to trust his instincts and quickly ran from the building just in time.

4. _____

The museum curator was shocked at the sight of coats and backpacks strewn on top of a precious antique love seat. "I am filled with consternation," the curator began his lecture to the confused students. "You must pay close attention to the museum's guidelines—no touching the displays."

Read the passage. Then, answer the questions on page 25.

# Mummies Have No Secrets

Mummies cannot hide their age. They cannot hide what they ate for their last meals or whether their families were wealthy or poor. Mummies, in fact, cannot hide much of anything from the anthropologists who study them.

The wrappings on a mummy and the artifacts found with the body reveal much about the social status of the person. For example, a mummy found in the Taklimakan Desert sported a bronze earring and leather boots. The decorations on these items showed that the mummy's people were skilled artisans. Other items found in the tombs of mummies include statues and jewelry or sometimes tools that the person might have used in life as a craftsperson.

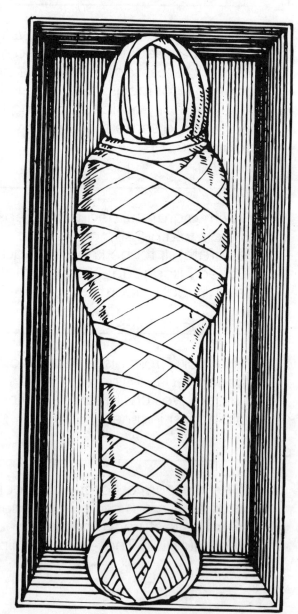

A mummy's body reveals even more clues. The contents of a mummy's digestive tract can be examined both chemically and microscopically, offering clues about the person's diet. When anthropologists studied the Iceman, a mummy found in Italy, they examined the contents of his intestines. They wanted to see what he ate in the hours before his death.

Organs and bones reveal details about the way the person died, too. Even if no flesh remains, bones and teeth can reveal the age of the person at death, as well as more details about diet, height, occupation, ethnicity, and social status. For example, a male mummy's worn front teeth might indicate that he used his teeth to hold a tool, freeing his hands for other work. In addition, since bone absorbs minerals during a person's life, a chemical study of the bones turns up information about the diet of the deceased person. If DNA can be extracted from the mummy, scientists can even determine the mummy's blood type.

Even death and 5,000 years of burial cannot hide a mummy's secrets. These secrets help contribute to what we know about ancient life and culture.

Use the passage on page 24 to answer the questions.

1. What is this passage about?

   _____

   _____

2. What is the purpose of this passage?

   A. to convince the reader that mummies are real

   B. to entertain the reader with a humorous story about the conversations of mummies

   C. to explain what can be learned from mummies

   D. to inform the reader about the mummies of ancient Egypt

3. List things a person can learn from a mummy.

   _____

   _____

   _____

   _____

   _____

4. Write a summary of the passage. In your summary, explain the meaning of the story's title.

   _____

   _____

   _____

   _____

   _____

   _____

Read the passage. Then, answer the questions on page 27.

# Alexis in Charge

Alexis was thrilled that her parents finally trusted her to be in charge of her four-year-old sister Chrissie. Chrissie could be a handful, but Alexis knew that she would be able to handle her when she was in charge.

After their parents left, Alexis and Chrissie sat down to watch TV. "We're going to watch my favorite show because I am in charge," Alexis announced. "I don't want to watch this show," Chrissie whined as she stood right in front of the TV and refused to move. Alexis dragged her to one side kicking and screaming. "You sit here because I am in charge," Alexis shouted over Chrissie's boisterous cries. Alexis tried to ignore her but Chrissie was crying so loudly Alexis couldn't even hear the TV, so she finally turned it off. "Okay, you win. Let's play a game," said Alexis. "Since I'm in charge, we'll play a word game," Alexis said as she grabbed the box filled with letter tiles. "The object of the game is to spell the longest word that you can with the tiles you have." Chrissie's face brightened as she grabbed her tiles with her chubby little fingers and spelled the word *cat*. "Well, that's good, but I can spell *monster* with my letters, so I win!" Alexis boasted proudly. Chrissie burst into tears again. "I don't want to play this game!" she cried with utter defeat.

"Okay, fine, it's dinner time anyway," Alexis explained as she put away the game.

"Can we have pizza?" Chrissie asked wiping away her tears.

"No, since I'm in charge, I get to choose what we are having and we are having macaroni and cheese," Alexis announced firmly enjoying the opportunity to be in charge.

Chrissie burst into tears, "I hate macaroni and cheese!"

"Alright, that's enough! You are going to bed. I am tired of your fussing and crying!" stated Alexis. Chrissie cried louder as she ran to her room. When Alexis went to check on Chrissie, Chrissie was sobbing on her bed.

"What's the matter with you?" Alexis said in a somewhat soothing tone. "You're never this much of a baby."

"I don't like it when you're in charge! You're mean!" Chrissie sobbed.

"Mean?" Alexis thought confused. "I watched my favorite TV show with her, and played my favorite game with her, and tried to fix her my favorite dinner . . ." It suddenly hit Alexis; she understood the problem and knew the fix.

"Why don't you choose your favorite book and I'll read it to you," Alexis suggested kindly. Chrissie beamed and ran and got a well-worn book from her bookshelf. She curled up close to Alexis and listened with awe as Alexis made the book come alive with her dramatic reading and voice inflections. The two girls read a couple of more books of Chrissie's choosing, and then colored in Chrissie's favorite coloring book. They both fell asleep watching one of Chrissie's favorite movies.

When their parents came home, they found Alexis and Chrissie asleep, with Alexis' arm around her younger sister. "I guess Alexis really is ready to be in charge," Mom said, smiling.

Use the passage on page 26 to answer the questions. Cite evidence from the story to support your responses.

1. What is this story about? Write a summary that answers who, what, when, where, and why.

   _____

   _____

   _____

   _____

   _____

2. How would you describe Alexis? Write a character summary that tells what she looks like, acts like, and how she feels.

   _____

   _____

   _____

   _____

   _____

3. How would you describe Chrissie? Write a character summary that tells what she looks like, acts like, and how she feels.

   _____

   _____

   _____

   _____

   _____

4. On a separate sheet of paper, write a personal narrative about a time when you were in charge. What lessons did you learn about leadership and being in charge?

Before reading the passage, complete question 1 on page 29. Then, read the passage and answer the remaining questions on page 29.

# A Hidden Wonder

The black, funnel-shaped cloud rising every day at sunset in the Chihuahuan Desert went largely ignored for thousands of years. Native Americans noticed it, but did not record any attempts to track its source. Cowboys in the region thought the cloud was smoke pouring from the earth, and avoided it.

In June of 1901, however, a cowboy named Jim White saw the large, black cloud as it poured out of the earth. He was curious and went to investigate. Instead of finding a volcano, as he had imagined, he discovered something equally amazing. It was a billowing mass of bats! Numbering in the millions, the bats flew out of a hole in the ground to go on their nighttime hunts for food. Jim White was the first known person in this remote area of New Mexico who saw the flight of the bats at close hand.

After the bats had flown away that evening, Jim crawled bravely down the gaping hole. It was pitch black, but Jim could sense that the tunnel led somewhere. Two days later, he returned with a lantern to explore further. The hole actually opened into two tunnels. One was obviously the home of the bats, and Jim decided to explore the second tunnel instead. It opened up into magnificent cave rooms filled with gigantic calcite formations. Jim was awestruck. He explored so long that his lantern went out, but he managed to refill it with just enough kerosene to find his way back to the entrance.

The next time Jim went to the cave, he brought a friend and supplies. They explored for three days and returned with descriptions that were so fantastic that few people believed them. The cowboys on nearby ranches and the 13 residents in the tiny town of Carlsbad treated Jim's stories as tall tales and nothing more.

After years of exploring the caves and finding no one to believe his stories, Jim decided to create his own tourist attraction. He built trails and installed railings along the paths he had found. One day in 1915, two men asked Jim for a tour. After seeing the incredible caves, the men returned with a professional photographer. Local doubts were finally put to rest by the photographs of the hidden beauty that Jim had discovered. All 13 residents of Carlsbad finally took a tour of the caves, which came to be known as Carlsbad Caverns.

In 1923, the government sent an inspector named Robert Holly to tour the caves. Later that year, the caverns were declared a national monument, and in 1930 they became a national park. Jim lived to see the Carlsbad Caverns become world-famous. Today, tourists can hike to and tour some of the 100 known caves in this huge natural wonder, thanks to the persistence and dedication of one cowboy from New Mexico.

Preview the passage on page 28 and answer question one. Then, read the passage on page 28 before completing the remainder of the page.

1. Reading the title and looking at the illustration on the page, what do you predict this passage will be about?

   _____

   _____

2. Write a summary telling what this passage is about. Tell who, what, when, where, and why.

   _____

   _____

   _____

   _____

3. Was your prediction correct? Explain.

   _____

   _____

4. Number the events in Jim White's life in order **1–7**.

   _____ Jim White takes Ray V. Davis into the caves.

   _____ Jim decides to build paths and install railings in the caves.

   _____ Jim White sees a black cloud rising from a hole in the ground.

   _____ Jim spends three days exploring the caves with a friend.

   _____ The residents of Carlsbad finally tour the caves with Jim White.

   _____ Carlsbad Caverns are declared a national park.

   _____ Carlsbad Caverns are declared a national monument.

Read the passage. Then, complete the chart on page 31.

# Vampire or Victim?

A man wandered in the dark night. During the day, he shrank from strong light. He avoided mirrors. He bared his teeth when approached by others or when he smelled garlic. When he died, horrified villages reported that his body still looked lifelike.

This true account from the 17th century sounds like something from a Hollywood horror film. But Spanish neurologist Juan Gomez-Alonso has a better explanation. Gomez-Alonso determined the man probably was the victim of rabies. The doctor noted the symptoms were remarkably similar to untreated rabies cases.

Legends about vampires first spread through Europe in the late 1600s. Since that time, books and movies have perpetuated these myths. Supposedly, vampires drink blood. Most vampires are portrayed as male. They have pale skin and staring eyes. They sleep during the day and wander at night. They can be warded off with garlic or mirrors. They are difficult to kill and can rise up even when people think they are dead.

Gomez-Alonso noticed that these kinds of vampire myths began circulating in Eastern Europe and Russia at about the same time that a rabies epidemic swept through the area. Another epidemic of rabies hit Hungary between 1721 and 1728, and suddenly stories of vampires were being published there. The doctor's research has correlated other incidents as well.

Research has shown more than seven times as many men as women contract rabies. Early symptoms include irritability and sleeplessness. As the disease progresses without treatment, some people will bite or attack others. About 25 percent of people infected with rabies will also bite other rabies victims. Strong light, reflections from mirrors, and strong odors will trigger spasms that seem to change the faces of sufferers. Also, throat spasms will make rabid people bare their teeth and froth at the mouth. During such a spasm, a person may bite his tongue or the inside of his cheek and the froth will have blood in it. Even in death, the disease of rabies changes normal human body responses. The illness makes the blood stay liquid longer. This keeps the skin looking pink and lifelike for longer than normal.

Because this disease was untreatable for hundreds of years and ran its course with the full range of symptoms, Gomez-Alonso concluded that "vampires" were actually victims of rabies. As people had to face the terrifying range of symptoms, they constructed their own stories to explain the dramatic changes in behavior of the disease's victims.

Name_____

Use the passage on page 30 to complete the chart.

| | Vampires | Rabies Victims |
|---|---|---|
| 1. Gender | A. _____ | B. _____ |
| 2. Appearance | A. _____ _____ | B. _____ _____ |
| 3. Behavior | A. _____ _____ _____ | B. _____ _____ _____ |
| 4. Death | A. _____ _____ _____ | B. _____ _____ _____ |

Read the passage. Then, answer the questions on page 33.

# Prairie Pioneers

In some of the most **remote**, least-populated places in the prairie, there are **bustling** towns that have existed for centuries. The founders of these towns built **intricate** systems of underground tunnels. The present-day inhabitants still use these tunnels; some are the **descendants** of the original pioneers and some are newer residents. On the **fringes** of these towns, enemies of the citizens lurk; sometimes they make sneak attacks on the downtown dwellers. These are the towns of the black-tailed prairie dogs, who have one of the tightest-knit communities in the animal kingdom. These fascinating and often misunderstood animals are worth a closer look.

Some people think that prairie dogs are related to domestic dogs, the dogs people have for pets, but prairie dogs are not even distantly related to domestic dogs. They get their name from their barking, which is how they communicate with each other and warn of **intruders**. Prairie dogs are actually sleek, plump members of the squirrel family. A prairie dog has small, rounded ears; a long, thin tail; short legs; and a yellow-gray or tawny coat.

Prairie dogs live on what is left of the great American prairie, which extends from Canada to northern Mexico. Because they eat grass and herbs, just like cattle, ranchers viewed prairie dogs as a threat to their cattle. On their own and with government agencies, ranchers mounted massive campaigns to get rid of the prairie dogs. As a result, the prairie dog population was reduced by 90 percent in the United States. Some breeds of prairie dogs now are considered threatened or endangered.

But there are still black-tailed prairie dogs plowing through the dirt, expanding their underground towns. Some of these towns extend for several miles and are home to thousands of prairie dogs. These towns are divided into wards, and are assigned to several extended families or coteries. Prairie dogs will defend their wards against all strangers, including other prairie dogs. Family members greet each other by a gesture that looks like kissing; but they are really checking each other's scent. They also show affection by playing together and grooming each other. Young prairie dogs actually play versions of tag and hide-and-seek with each other.

When a prairie dog sees danger, usually in the form of a bird of prey, a coyote, or a badger, it stands on its hind legs and gives a shrill warning bark. Other prairie dogs dive underground as soon as the warning is given. The opening shafts that lead to the underground city plunge down between 10 and 12 feet (3–3.7 m). When prairie dogs dig new tunnels, they use the dirt to construct crater-shaped cones around the entrances.

These barriers keep out water. The wards include networks of tunnels, including turning bays (for turning around) and apartment-like chambers.

If you're ever driving through the prairie and you think the rolling expanse of land is boring, just think of the thriving city that might lie just below the grass.

Use the passage on page 32 to answer the questions.

1. What are three main differences between prairie dogs and domestic dogs?

   _____

   _____

   _____

2. How do the lives of prairie dogs differ from wild members of the dog family, such as wolves?

   _____

   _____

   _____

3. What conclusions can you draw about prairie dogs because of the way in which their underground cities are built?

   _____

   _____

   _____

4. Define the following words as they are used in this passage. Use context clues or a dictionary if needed.

   remote: _____

   bustling: _____

   intricate: _____

   descendants: _____

   fringes: _____

   intruders: _____

Read the passage. Then, answer the questions on page 35.

# First Job

Are you the kind of person who thinks ahead to when you will have your first job? What kind of job will you look for? Read the descriptions of three open positions at a grocery store. This grocery store also offers a service that allows customers to order their groceries on an Internet site.

## HIRING GROCERY STAGER

Duties include preparing a customer's order for delivery and making sure that orders are properly packed in numbered bins and ready for our delivery drivers to load and deliver during the appropriate time slot as requested by the customer.

We are looking for a friendly, people-oriented individual with strong communication skills, a high level of attention to detail, and superior customer service in a fast-paced environment. We offer excellent advancement opportunities with a rapidly expanding Internet grocery shopping and delivery business, consistent raises, flexible scheduling, incentives and bonuses, and a casual work environment. Benefits include medical and dental insurance, 401K savings plan, and employee discount.

## HIRING GROCERY STOCKER

Duties include unpacking, organizing, and shelving new products. Stockers also gather all damaged and expired products from the shelves and prepare the products for return to the manufacturers.

We are looking for individuals with a strong work ethic and the ability to work independently. Hours for this position will be from 11:00 pm to 5:00 am. We offer excellent benefits including medical and dental insurance, 401K savings plan, and employee discounts.

## CASHIER

Duties include using a scanner and cash register to check out customers in a friendly and efficient manner. Cashiers need to be able to handle money and count back change.

We are looking for a friendly, people-oriented individual with strong communication skills, a high level of attention to detail, and superior customer service in a fast-paced environment. We offer excellent advancement opportunities, consistent raises, flexible scheduling, incentives and bonuses, and excellent benefits.

Use the passage on page 34 to answer the questions. Cite evidence from the text to support your responses.

1. How are the three positions alike?

   _____

   _____

   _____

2. How are the three positions different?

   _____

   _____

   _____

3. Which of these positions would best fit your personality?

   _____

   _____

   _____

4. Write a job description for your "perfect" job.

   _____

   _____

   _____

   _____

   _____

   _____

   _____

Read the passage. Then, complete the activities on page 37.

# The Smile

Henry was in a pickle and this was peculiar because Henry was never **in a pickle**. He was extremely organized and planned everything **to a tee** so that he didn't get into the **spot** that he found himself in today.

A week ago his friend Shauna came up to him after math class to ask if Henry would be willing to care for Mitzi, her dog, while she went out of town with her dad for the weekend. Shauna was one of the prettiest girls in eighth grade and just the sight of her caused Henry to become **tongue-tied**. Henry tried his best to say no because a dog was not in his plans, but Shauna could be very **persuasive**. She met every one of his excuses with a convincing **rebuttal**, not to mention her smile that could melt stone. Before he knew it, Henry had fallen victim to Shauna's charms and was agreeing to take care of Mitzi for the weekend.

This morning Shauna called to say she was bringing Mitzi right over. When Shauna and her dad drove up, Mitzi hopped out of the car, and scampered over to Henry, and smiled up at him. Well, it looked like a smile to Henry. "Oh, no she is a charmer just like Shauna," Henry thought to himself. "I've heard that dogs take on the looks and the characteristics of the their owners. This is **uncanny**!"

" She likes you," remarked Shauna flashing her own toothy smile.

"Here's her stuff." Shauna handed over dog dishes, food, cage, leash, cushion, and puppy toys. After giving a few instructions, Shauna rode off with her dad.

"Well, Mitzi, it's you and me. Are you hungry?" began Henry nervously. He and the dog entered the house where they made their way to the kitchen. Henry set out a mat and placed the water and food dishes on them. Mitzi smiled at Henry again. When she was done eating, Henry went into the living room to watch some TV. Mitzi trotted behind him, leaped into his lap, and smiled at him.

Henry loved having Mitzi curled up on his lap. He never thought holding a warm animal could be so comforting. After the show was over, Henry said, "You want to go for a walk?" Henry understood the little dog's wagging tail and shaking to mean yes. So Henry grabbed Mitzi's leash, and the two were off for a **invigorating** stroll.

That night Henry tried to put Mitzi in her cage in the kitchen to sleep, but Mitzi let out a howl. He entered the kitchen, opened the cage door, scooped up the whimpering Mitzi, and quietly brought Mitzi to his room. As he reached over to scratch her head, he saw her smile again. "You know how to charm me don't you?" Mitzi just put her head on her paws and smiled.

Use the passage on page 36 to complete the activities.

1.  Place the following events in order **1-8** as they occurred in the story.

    _____ Henry agreed to watch Mitzi for the weekend.

    _____ Henry put Mitzi in her cage in the kitchen to sleep.

    _____ Henry fed Mitzi.

    _____ Shauna asked Henry to watch her dog.

    _____ Mitzi curled up on Henry's lap while he watched TV.

    _____ Henry brought Mitzi to his room to sleep.

    _____ Henry took Mitzi for a walk.

    _____ Shauna dropped Mitzi off at Henry's house.

2.  What did Henry mean when he thought the resemblance between Shauna and Mitzi was **uncanny**?

    _____

    _____

    _____

3.  Define the following words as they are used in the story. Use context clues and a dictionary if needed.

    spot: _____

    persuasive: _____

    rebuttal: _____

    invigorating: _____

4.  Write the meaning of each idiom used in this story.

    in a pickle: _____

    to a tee: _____

    tongue-tied: _____

Read the passage. Then, complete the activities on page 39.

# The Storm

Throughout the afternoon Trent felt an **ominous boding** sensation. During research time in the media center, the air was thick and sweaty. When he worked with his study team planning a math presentation, the classroom was **stiflingly** hot. The school day fortunately came to a close, and he escaped outdoors to catch whatever breeze was there.

His walk home wasn't long, just four blocks, but today's mood was eerie. The clouds were charcoal gray and darkening quickly and three large raindrops splattered to the sidewalk as Trent started his walk home.

"It's going to be a soaker," thought Trent. Not that he minded getting wet. It might cool him down a bit.

Now the street lights switched on. A whispering stir of wind rattled the maple seeds in the trees. A sudden gust of wind nearly pulled the cap from Trent's head. He clapped his hand over his cap just in time.

A growing, rolling rumble of thunder told Trent that the storm was coming soon. The crisp clap of thunder startled him just the same. Pulling his backpack strap tight and shoving his cap firmly on, Trent began his mad dash toward home.

Now the wind howled. Lightning slashed into a spruce tree two houses ahead. The needled branch slipped down and crashed inches in front of Trent.

"Whoa!" Trent shouted at the branch but more at the glistening silver wall of rain water speeding at him. In less time than it takes to **flinch**, the **gale** blasted into Trent. It soaked him to the skin instantly.

Breathing in particles of **precipitation**, Trent picked up the pace.

The wind roared on. Branches cracked and tumbled about. A mighty oak tree blew over across a power line which sparked as it stretched and split.

Trent was soaked and fearful and winded and shaken. He ran through the storm. The last two blocks.

Fumbling with the key, he stood in the wind-whipped wet and fiddled with the lock until he gained entrance.

Trent dropped his backpack, took off his jacket, and kicked off his soggy shoes.

Trent bounded into the kitchen and stopped. There on the floor crouched Pepper. The tail-tapping dog was wet and frightened. She whimpered and trembled.

"Hey, girl. Why are you wet, huh?"

And then he remembered. He had let Pepper outside that morning and forgot to let her back in. The storm frightened her into such a frenzy that she jumped through the screened door off the kitchen.

"Aw, poor girl. It's alright," soothed Trent, petting her. "We're safe now."

Use the passage on page 38 to complete the activities.

1. Place the following events in order **1–10** as they occurred in the story.

_____ A sudden gust of wind nearly pulled the cap from Trent's head.

_____ Trent assured Pepper they were safe.

_____ Lightening struck a spruce tree.

_____ Throughout the afternoon Trent felt an ominous boding sensation.

_____ A branch crashed inches away from Trent.

_____ Trent arrived home.

_____ The clouds were gray and darkening quickly.

_____ Trent found his wet dog whimpering.

_____ The clap of thunder startled Trent.

_____ A tree fell on to a power line causing a spark.

2. Define the following words as they are used in the story. Use context clues and a dictionary if needed.

ominous: _____

boding: _____

stifling: _____

flinch: _____

gale: _____

precipitation: _____

3. On a separate sheet of paper or on the computer, write a personal narrative about a time that you experienced an extreme weather condition.

Read the passage. Then, complete the activities on page 41.

# Pajamas

It was Tony's fault; he started it when he took hold of my increasingly thin, worn pajamas and yanked. R-r-r-rip!

"Hey, what are you doing?" I protested.

"Aw, come on, Nick, you know Grandma's making us new ones. She always does this time of year."

"Yeah, you're right." I admitted grabbing hold of the elastic waistband of Tony's pajamas and giving it a well-deserved tug—rip! I had to admit that felt good. After all, we'd get new ones. We played tug-of-war with our pajamas as the rope—with our pajamas losing each time. But it didn't matter, since we'd be getting new ones.

On Saturday afternoon our family piled into the car and headed to Grandma and Grandpa's house. As we entered the house the smells of all our familiar foods, desserts, and breads were thick. We were greeted by aunts, uncles, cousins, and of course Grandma and Grandpa.

After dinner the cousins would all gather to open presents. Uncle Dale loved to tease us. Just when we thought we were going to open our gifts he would ask that Grandpa tell one of his stories—you know the kind that can go on and on. As Grandpa started his story, Uncle Dale would grin and look over at Tony and me, and wink! Finally Grandma would intervene and hand each of us a nicely wrapped package. That's how it happened every year since I could remember—just like getting pajamas every year. There were just some things in life you could always count on.

Right on cue, just as always Grandma interrupted Grandpa and stated that it was time to open presents. She handed each of the kids their gift and then said, "Ready? Open!" and together we all tore into the package. For the first time in forever, I was actually looking forward to my new pair of pajamas since the ones I had were now just rags. As Tony and I opened our boxes, we smiled knowingly at each other. But instead of finding our pajamas neatly folded in the box as they always were, we found two pairs of socks, a knitted beanie, and a scarf.

"Thanks, Grandma!" we said as enthusiastically as we could manage. We were confused and rosy-cheeked. Grandma never made us another pair of pajamas. Later that night, when Mom discovered the state of our pajamas, she was not happy with us. "It was Tony's fault," I tried to convince her but she would have none of it. The next day she took us to the store and we bought some new pajamas, with our own allowance.

Use the passage on page 40 to complete the activities.

1. Place the following events in order **1–12** as they occurred in the story.

   _____ The boys played tug-of-war with their pajamas.

   _____ When we opened the packages we found socks, a beanie, and a scarf.

   _____ Grandpa would tell stories.

   _____ Nick ripped the waistband of Tony's pajamas.

   _____ Mom took us to buy store-bought pajamas using our own allowance.

   _____ After dinner the cousins gathered to open presents.

   _____ Tony ripped Nick's pajamas.

   _____ Grandma stated that it was time to open presents.

   _____ Uncle Dale asked Grandpa to tell one of his stories.

   _____ Mom discovered the state of our pajamas.

   _____ The family piled in the car and went to Grandma and Grandpa's house.

   _____ We tore open the packages.

2. Write the sequence of events as they construct the plot of the story.

   Problem: _____

   _____

   Rising Action: _____

   _____

   Turning Point: _____

   _____

   Falling Action: _____

   _____

   Resolution: _____

   _____

Read the passage. Then, complete the activities on page 43.

# Queen of the Heap

Life when I was a kid was great! Whenever I had a hankering for something to do, all I had to do was go outside. You see, my family lived in the country, and I had the whole world for a playground and lots of kids to play with. The Benson twins lived just across the road from us and the Zimmermans and Averys lived within easy walking distance.

Wintertime provided an especially magical play yard. We could sled down the hill behind the Zimmerman's house, build snow forts behind the Benson's chicken coop, skate on the Avery's frozen pond, or play Hide-and-Seek throughout the neighborhood. We could sled for hours, flying down the hill on our steel-runner sleds. My older sister Liv was often the ringleader—whatever we did, she could do better. If I landed safely after a fly over our jumbo ski jump, she'd be sure to jump farther and land better. If we built a snow fort, she'd build a castle. If someone broke her record for sliding the longest distance, she'd break that record anew by another good ten feet.

One year my dad got a snowmobile. We loved flying through the fields on that noisy contraption with the wintry winds whipping all sensation from our air-exposed cheeks. Our eyes would water great tears, which collected and froze on our ice-hardened scarves. Dad rigged a toggle to the rear of the snowmobile so we could be pulled on skis and sleds.

Liv, of course, thought she was queen of the snowmobile; and she probably was. She could lazy-eight that snow machine with a clean cut Scott Hamilton couldn't match. She could slalom through the young apple trees better than Peek-a-Boo Street. We'd marvel at her performance, more than a little jealous of her mobile magic.

But on this particular day, the hill was faster and slicker than ever and we loved it! We were enjoying sledding down the hill when Liv came roaring up on the snowmobile, scattering us like milkweed seeds. Suddenly and without notice Liv lost her balance and toppled off the snowmobile which was speedin' near 57 mph. Well, that snowmobile wobbled to the left; it leaned to the right; it tilted to the left again, and...tipped over.

Somehow, Liv had frozen the throttle in place and that machine sped in circles on its side, completing donuts around the fallen form of my stunned-to-silence sister. Around and around sped the riderless steed. Finally tired of its mundane donut-making, the tread-spinnin' machine righted itself, got its bearings, and roared across the gravel road toward the twins' cow barn; but before reaching the barn it slammed head-on into a large, pungent pile of manure. Its engine cut out with one mighty whoomp!

Liv rose to her feet and flashed her haughty, queenly smile at us and crowed, "Bet'cha couldn't do that trick!"

She was right, of course. We couldn't.

Use the passage on page 42 to determine what is the cause and effect for each pair of sentences. Write **C** if the sentence is the cause or **E** if the sentence is the effect.

1. _____ Life was great!

2. _____ My family lived in the country and I had the whole world as my playground.

3. _____ The Benson twins lived just across the road from us and the Zimmermans and Averys lived within easy walking distance.

4. _____ I had lots of kids to play with.

5. _____ Liz lost her balance on the snowmobile.

6. _____ She toppled off the snowmobile.

7. _____ The snowmobile sped in circles on its side.

8. _____ Liz had frozen the throttle in place.

9. _____ The snowmobile slammed head-on into a pile of manure.

10. _____ The engine cut out.

11. Write about something that happened in your life that caused something else to happen.

   _____

   _____

   _____

12. Even if the author had not stated "my family lived in the country," what other descriptions in the passage would have indicated the setting?

   _____

   _____

   _____

Read the passage. Then, answer the questions on page 45.

# A Lost Language

*Manhattan. Rockaway.* If you have ever spoken these words, you were speaking a language that is nearly lost. These words come from the Munsee Delaware language that was once spoken by the Delaware Indians of Long Island. Today, only a handful of people are fluent in this language. Canadian linguist John O'Meara worries that the language may become extinct. Only a few people speak the language fluently and with no specific program to preserve the language, O'Meara doubts that the language will survive.

When O'Meara first began studying Munsee Delaware, he made dozens of recordings of the speakers who remained. Someday listening to those recordings may be the only way to hear Munsee Delaware spoken. O'Meara also wrote a dictionary to help preserve the language.

Thomas Jefferson studied the Munsee Delaware language when they were still living in Ohio. The Munsee Delaware Indians had been driven westward by Dutch settlers. Many Munsee Delaware lived in eastern Ohio by the 1780s, when Jefferson visited them. He suggested that nearly all of what is now Ohio be turned into a reservation. His suggestion was ignored; and soon afterward, a massacre of 90 Delaware drove the group out of Ohio and into Michigan and then Canada.

Today, only about 300–500 Munsee Delaware populate the reservation. Only about ten of those are fluent in the language of their ancestors; but with O'Meara's dictionary and language programs on the Munsee Delaware reservations, there is hope that this language will not be lost.

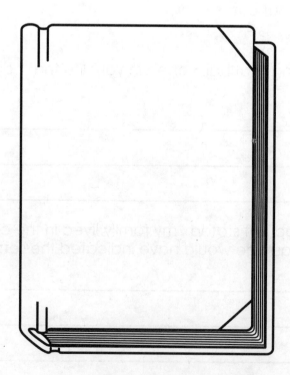

Use the passage on page 44 to answer the questions.

1. What is John O'Meara's primary concern? (Cause)

   _____

   _____

   _____

2. What did O'Meara do to affect his concern? (Effect)

   _____

   _____

   _____

3. What caused the Munsee Delaware to move westward to Ohio?

   _____

   _____

   _____

4. What was the effect of Thomas Jefferson's suggestion to turn all of Ohio into a reservation?

   _____

   _____

   _____

5. What caused the Munsee Delaware to move to Michigan and Canada?

   _____

   _____

   _____

Read the letter. Then, answer the questions on page 47.

# A Sad Day in History

November 25, 1963

Dear Joanne,

Today was the saddest day in American history. My family crowded around the small television set in our living room watching the funeral of the most beloved president the United States of America has ever had. What will this country do without this great leader?

The casket was pulled to the church on a caisson, which is usually used to pull a cannon. Like so many details of the funeral, the idea of using the caisson was taken from the funeral of Abraham Lincoln. Before the death of President Kennedy, President Lincoln was the only US President to hold the dubious privilege of being assassinated. Both events were tragic, but people then could not have felt the shock that we do today.

Mrs. Kennedy wore a black veil over her hair and stood bravely holding the hands of her two young children, now fatherless. I don't think I will ever forget the muffled drums, the trumpet playing taps, or the riderless horse, which symbolized a fallen leader. It was a more powerful symbol than the missing jet fighter from the V-formation that flew over the heads of those who attended the funeral. But the most moving tribute was when little John-John, the president's four-year-old son, saluted the casket in which his father lay. There was not a dry eye at the funeral or in our home. My mother and aunts cried. My father said the funeral made him feel old and tired. Tonight, I feel tired too . . . and sad . . . and scared. Every person in the United States is scared tonight. How can something this awful happen and to a man so young?

Your pen pal,
Ginny

Use information from the letter on page 46 to decide if the statements are facts or opinions. Write **F** if the statement is fact or **O** if the statement is opinion.

1. _____ "A Sad Day in History" is about the funeral of President John F. Kennedy.

2. _____ The funeral of John F. Kennedy was the saddest day in US history.

3. _____ John F. Kennedy's funeral was based on the funeral of Abraham Lincoln.

4. _____ It was fitting that Kennedy's funeral be based on the death of another great leader.

5. _____ The riderless horse was the most powerful symbol of a fallen leader at the funeral.

6. _____ Another symbol of a fallen leader was a missing fighter jet from an overhead formation.

7. _____ The people of 1963 were more shocked by a presidential assassination than people of the Civil War era.

8. _____ On the evening of November 25, 1963, everyone in America felt sad and tired.

9. _____ Mrs. Kennedy had two children.

10. In your opinion, which was the greater loss, the death of Abraham Lincoln or the death of John F. Kenney? Research to find out more about the climate of the country at the times of these deaths. On a separate sheet of paper or on the computer, write an essay stating your opinion and support your opinion with facts.

Read the passage. Then, answer the questions on page 49.

# Tramp Art

A man stood outside a general store on a day in the mid-1930s. He unwrapped the tattered flour sack from around a wooden object. Holding up the object for inspection by the first store patron who appeared, he asked, "Could you use a picture frame?"

The frame was an example of tramp art. The man had fashioned the frame from thin layers of wood. Tiny V-shaped notches decorated the edges of each quarter-inch layer. He cut each layer narrower than the one beneath it, and then stacked them. Glue held the layers together, and a dab of yellow paint dotted each notch. The notches and thin layers created an intricate, geometrical design.

This folk-art form probably began in Europe, where fathers taught their sons the craft. In America, most tramp art was created during the Depression. Desperate men known as tramps left their homes and roamed the country, vainly looking for work. Rather than accept handouts of food to survive, some chose to make objects to sell. Poverty forced the artists to scavenge wood and glue for their projects. Cigar boxes and fruit crates often furnished the wood. Many tramp artists created picture frames, but some also built bigger objects such as desks and chests. Some artists smoothed and burnished their wooden pieces to a deep luster, and others also painted them when they could scavenge small amounts of paint.

Today, folk art is increasingly popular and tramp art from the 1930s has become valuable in the antiques market. A group of formerly homeless men recently formed an artists' group to make and sell new tramp art. By working together, these men have been luckier than tramps of the Depression. They have built a thriving business and have been able to buy homes for themselves. When you see a piece of tramp art, old or new, remember that this art grew out of a struggle for survival and the desire to express oneself through art.

Use information from the passage on page 48 to decide if the statements are facts or opinions. Write **F** is the statement is fact or **O** if the statement is opinion.

1. _____ During the Depression many people were unable to find jobs.

2. _____ Tramp art is one of the most beautiful crafts of the 20th century.

3. _____ The best tramp art has intricate, geometrical designs.

4. _____ Tramps scavenged materials to create their art.

5. _____ The notches and thin layers created an intricate, geometrical design.

6. _____ Tramp art probably began in Europe.

7. _____ Tramps created tramp art because they didn't want to work.

8. _____ Tramps used old cigar boxes and fruit crates to create their art.

9. Look on the Internet to see samples of tramp art. Then, write a paragraph stating your opinion of tramp art. Is it a type of art you would purchase? Explain.

_____

_____

_____

_____

_____

_____

_____

_____

_____

_____

Read the passage. Then, answer the questions on page 51.

# Golden Words

Rose O'Neal Greenhow sighed. She picked up the pen and leaned forward, writing the Secretary of State's address at the top of a sheet of stationery. She had just begun the letter that she hoped would result in her freedom.

She protested that she had been unfairly imprisoned. Jailers held her and her daughter in Washington's Old Capitol Prison. "And thus for a period of seven days, I, with my little child, was placed absolutely at the mercy of men without character or responsibility," Greenhow wrote in her 1861 letter.

Nicknamed "Wild Rose" when she was still a child, she grew up to be a famous Washington hostess and Confederate spy. As the Civil War loomed, she spoke often and passionately about her views. She opposed Lincoln's decisions.

When war broke out, Greenhow did not stop talking. She just did it in secret. She worked with devious skill as a Confederate spy. Her position as hostess put her in contact with many important people, and she used her charm and position to obtain and overhear information. So important was the information she leaked that some historians credit her with two important Confederate victories early in the war. She managed to get information to the Confederates even after her imprisonment, hiding messages in women visitors' hair and other unlikely places.

Greenhow's letter did not win her immediate release, but she was eventually let out of prison. She was exiled to the Confederacy. From there she traveled to England, where she used her skill with words to drum up sympathy for treacherous Confederate causes. She also wrote her prison memoirs, and her publishers paid her in gold.

Those golden words proved to be her undoing. When she was returning from England on the Condor, a Union gunboat pursued the vessel. The Condor ran aground. Greenhow escaped in a rowboat, but that boat capsized. The weight of the gold she was carrying dragged Greenhow down. She drowned, killed by the weight of her own words.

Use the passage on page 50 to answer the questions. Cite evidence from the article to support your responses.

1.  What is the author's purpose for writing this article?

    A.  to entertain the reader with stories from the Civil War

    B.  to convince the reader that Greenhow got what she deserved

    C.  to describe the conflict between the Confederacy and the Union

    D.  to inform the reader about the poor quality of prisons during the Civil War

2.  Write four adjectives or phrases that the author uses to influence the reader's opinion.

    _____

    _____

    _____

    _____

3.  The author could have written the article without including Greenhow's nickname. Why do you think the author included this detail?

    _____

    _____

4.  Why do you think that the author chose to add the detail that it was the weight of Greenhow's payment in gold that contributed to her death?

    _____

    _____

5.  How does your impression of Greenhow's imprisonment change from the beginning to the end of the article? Explain.

    _____

    _____

    _____

Read the passage. Then, answer the questions on page 53.

# Doctor Anna

Anna Pierce Hobbs Bigsby was a determined woman. In the early nineteenth century, women performed most of the nursing at home for their own family members, but Bigsby wanted to do more than nurse. She wanted to be a doctor.

Born in 1808, she had become a pioneer at the age of 16 when her family moved to Illinois. The wilderness of Illinois had few doctors, and Anna wanted to serve her community. But in the nineteenth century, few medical schools admitted women. When Anna finally located a school in Philadelphia, the school limited the courses that she could take. Fortunately, no school could limit her curiosity and determination.

When Doctor Anna, as she came to be known, returned home in 1828, she soon faced an epidemic that was sweeping through southern Illinois. Both people and animals were the victims of a mysterious illness called "milk sickness." They walked stiffly, trembled, and became increasingly weak. Many died. Anna lost her mother and sister-in-law to milk sickness. Another resident of Illinois, Abraham Lincoln, lost his mother in this same epidemic.

Many settlers blamed witches for the illness, but Doctor Anna set aside this ridiculous explanation. She was determined to use her medical training to find the true cause of the disease. Her notes soon revealed that milk sickness became serious in the summer, and then abated after the first frost in the autumn. Although horses, goats, and pigs sometimes were affected, cattle were the most frequent animal victims. Doctor Anna wondered if something that the cattle ate caused the illness. She also noted that people might be contracting the illness from drinking tainted milk or eating tainted meat from the cattle.

Anna began doing field work in the truest sense of the word: she headed to the fields and observed grazing cattle. One day when she was following a herd, she met a Shawnee woman. As they talked, the Shawnee woman showed the doctor a plant called white snakeroot. The Native American suggested that this poisonous plant might be causing the problem.

Doctor Anna set up an experiment to test the Shawnee woman's theory. After feeding white snakeroot to a calf, she was able to prove that the plant caused milk sickness. Then this energetic doctor began a campaign to convince farmers in the area to get rid of the plants. As a result, many lives were saved.

Most resources do not list Doctor Anna's discovery of the source of milk sickness. At the time of her death in 1869, neither Anna nor the anonymous Shawnee woman had received any credit for this important medical breakthrough. But Doctor Anna had been determined to stop people from dying of milk sickness, and that is exactly what she achieved.

Use the passage on page 52 to answer the questions.

1. What was the author's purpose in writing the passage?

   A. to prove to the reader the Doctor Anna was the best doctor in the early nineteenth century

   B. to provide evidence to show that Doctor Anna was a very determined woman

   C. to entertain the reader with an interesting story about an epidemic

   D. to persuade young women to become doctors

2. What words does the author use to describe Doctor Anna?

   _____

   _____

3. Cite three examples that the author provides that show Anna as determined.

   _____

   _____

   _____

4. Write a brief biographical sketch of Doctor Anna. Do not include any opinions.

   _____

   _____

   _____

   _____

   _____

   _____

   _____

   _____

Read the passage. Then, answer the questions on page 55.

# Take a Hike

Having a bad day? Did your friends make fun of your new shirt? Did your mother make an appointment for you with the dentist? Did your first-period teacher give you a pop quiz? Maybe you ought to **take a hike**.

Don't run away from your problems. Just get outside! A new science called *biophilia* suggests that humans have a built-in need to spend time outside. Spending time outdoors lowers blood pressure and causes breathing to slow and deepen. The effect is so profound that some studies have shown that patients recover from surgery faster if they can look out their windows at nature views. Additional studies have shown that dental patients are calmer if they can gaze at a poster of a nature scene above their heads.

For maximum calming effect, studies encourage people to head to a park with green lawns and low, squat trees dotting the landscape. Across all cultures, people prefer grasslands dotted with trees. Scientists point out the similarities of this kind of landscape to the savannas where humans first lived before populating the rest of the world. Many of our parks look like savannas where humans first lived. Even in past ages, royalty often designed their play spaces with wide expanses of lawn shaded by low trees with wide-spread branches. They imported large animals to colonize these savanna-like areas. According to Professor Stephen R. Kellert of Yale School of Forestry and Environmental Studies, biophilia might also explain why attendance at zoos is higher than the total attendance at all professional football, baseball, and basketball games.

With evidence like this it only makes sense to take a hike, hiking gets you away from your problems and helps you reduce your stress.

Use the passage on page 54 to answer the questions.

1.  What is the author's purpose for writing this passage?

    A.  to prove that everyone has a bad day occasionally

    B.  to persuade the reader to visit the zoo

    C.  to persuade the reader to get outside

    D.  to inform the reader on the calming effect of a football game

2.  Who is the audience of this passage?

    A.  doctors and others in the medical field

    B.  parents

    C.  teenagers

    D.  patients recovering from surgery

3.  What techniques does the author use to keep the reader interested in reading the passage?

    _____

    _____

    _____

4.  How would this passage be different if it was an article in a medical journal?

    _____

    _____

    _____

5.  What does the idiom "take a hike" mean?

    _____

6.  Did the author convince you to take a hike to solve your problems? Explain.

    _____

    _____

Read the passage. Then, complete the graphic organizers on page 57.

# The Visit

I was so nervous. I hadn't been back to the United States since I was born and though I knew of many of the people we would see, I didn't *know* them. They were family and friend who had immigrated there years before. We had not. My parents only were there for about four years so that my father could go to school there. There was only one family we would see on our trip that I do remember—Abbie's family. Abbie was my best friend in fourth grade. Her family came to our country so her parents could study at the university here. Abbie and I were so close that year. We learned our times tables together, watched videos, talked about those stupid boys, and played soccer. We shared our secret thoughts and our young, naive dreams. We used to say that we were twins because our names were so similar, Abbie and Anna, although the differences in our skin color didn't fool anyone.

But that was three years ago and people change. When she left, we promised to keep in touch, but we both got busy and the letters became fewer. I wondered if Abbie still told those silly garlic jokes. I wondered if we would have anything in common any more.

When we arrived in the states, we made our rounds to visit the people Mom and Dad knew. I got hugs and kisses from "uncles" and "aunts" I only knew through letters. It's kind of weird being hugged by people you don't know, but I get through it by imagining I'm hugging someone's pet. I probably won't ever see these people again anyway. My dad was also invited to lecture at two colleges. He got a lot of praise, I fidgeted.

Oh! I really wanted to see Abbie. I wanted to have back those fun times we once had. Giggle under the bedcovers at night. Laugh at my dad's silly jokes. Pretend that we were sisters. But then, I thought some more. What if we had nothing to talk about? I fidgeted some more.

We drove to Abbie's town, stopping about an hour away to call them to let them know we were on our way. When we got to their house, the whole family was outside waiting for us. Both her parents, her brother Alexis, and...Abbie! She was taller (but so was I). Her face was thinner than it used to be, but her smile was the same.

We said hi and hugged kind of tight, but kind of foreign, too. Then we went inside and sat down. Our parents talked about our families and mutual friends and how we had changed. Abbie and I just sat and smiled. Awkwardly. Silently. Then Abbie got a sick feeling in her stomach and had to lie down. I got a sick stomach but didn't tell anyone. It was a lousy visit. Things were different; we were different.

I'm glad I'm back in Costa Rica. Americans are alright, I guess. But it hurts to be strangers with someone who was my best friend.

Use the passage on page 56 to complete the graphic organizers.

1. What can you infer about the author?

2. What can you infer about Abbie?

3. What can you infer about the author's dad?

4. What can you infer about the author's visit to the United States?

Read the passage. Then, answer the questions on page 59.

# No Ordinary Storm

From her lifeguard station at the shallow end of the pool, Becky noticed clouds gathering in the sky. By the time she took a break at 2:30, the wind was picking up and the sky was darkening. The pool manager announced over the loudspeaker that the pool was closing immediately, due to a severe weather warning. He asked everyone to head to the safety of home before the storm hit.

All of the swimmers had left by 3:30 except for Jessica's neighbor, eight-year-old Zack. Zack's mother had dropped him off at the pool while she ran several errands. She had planned to pick him up later, but the storm was approaching fast. Jessica decided that she would drop Zack off on her way home. She quickly sent Zack's mom a text and taped a note for her on the door of the pool office just in case she didn't get the text and headed out with Zack in tow.

The minute Jessica and Zack left the parking lot, it was clear that this was no ordinary storm. The wind came in strong blasts, the storm clouds were dense and dark, and the sky had turned an eerie green. The rain hit just as Jessica turned onto her street, coming down in sheets and making it hard to see clearly. Jessica said, "Zack, I'm going to take you to my house. We need to get inside right away, and your house is farther away than mine."

She pressed the garage-door opener, but nothing happened. The electricity was out. The front door was only a few feet away, but the wind was so strong that Jessica and Zack had to fight their way out of the car and into the house. Jessica held Zack's hand firmly. The door was heavy with the pressure of the wind. Finally, it opened, but it was wrenched out of Jessica's hand and it slammed against the side of the house. The window shattered. Jessica grabbed Zack's hand and pulled him inside; her only thought was to get to a safe place.

Remembering everything she could from her emergency training, Jessica dragged Zack to the basement stairs. Her heart was pounding. The stairwell was pitch black without the overhead light. After what seemed like hours, Jessica felt the door to the storage closet under the stairs. "We'll be safe in here, Zack," she said, trying to sound calm and reassuring. They had just gotten inside when everything went deadly quiet for a moment. Then they could hear the sound of glass breaking and the furniture being tossed against the walls by the wind. A deafening roar, like the sound of a train, filled their ears. "Tuck your head under your arms," Jessica yelled to Zack.

After a final crash, the lifeguard and her charge felt drops of rain on their arms. They saw a flash of lightening through a crack in the ceiling. The sound of the storm grew distant. Jessica began to breathe easier. She and Zack were safe, and what a story they would have to tell!

Name_____

Read the passage on page 58. Then, answer the questions. Cite evidence from the story to support your responses.

1. What is the first indication that the storm in this story was going to be a bad one?

   _____

   _____

   _____

2. Why did Jessica decide to take Zack home?

   _____

   _____

   _____

3. Do you feel Jessica made the right decision?

   _____

   _____

   _____

4. When did Jessica know she and Zack were safe?

   _____

   _____

   _____

5. What kind of storm occurs in the story?

   _____

   _____

   _____

Read the passage. Then, answer the questions on page 61.

# Not Fair!

Katie was steaming again. It always was the same; Princess Grace, as Katie liked to call her older sister, could do no wrong, at least not in their mother's eyes. Princess Grace was attending the nearby college and living in the dorm, but you would never know as often as she swooped in and out of the house. Yesterday, she came home and spent the night camping out in front of the TV all evening so Katie and her best friend Kimberly couldn't watch the DVD they had rented. She left this morning, taking Katie's winter coat with her!

"Mom, I need another coat, Princess Grace took mine with her without even asking," I complained in my usual tone to my mother, who in her usual tone responded, "Oh, that's right Grace needs a new coat. I forgot she lost her coat at the end of last winter; I will have to go buy her one today."

"Hello?" Katie thought, "The girl took *my* coat and you're worried *she* might get cold?" Katie stomped off to her room pouting as usual about being treated like the ugly stepsister, even though she wasn't ugly and wasn't a stepsister.

Katie was going to the mall with Kimberly later that afternoon so she quickly sent Grace a text—"Bring back my coat . . . or else"—adding a grimacing emoji. There was no responding text. "How dare she not even respond," Katie thought indignantly. "Well, she's been warned," Katie thought smugly as she began to plan her revenge.

As Mom was leaving to run some errands she reminded Katie to take the dog out. Poor Katie not only had to walk the dog on a freezing cold day, she had do it wearing her dad's bulking sweatshirt and her mom's ugly, out-dated scarf. Katie felt and looked a little like Tiny Tim giving her more incentive in planning her revenge against the princess.

When Katie got back from walking the dog and there was still no response from Grace to her text, she thought, "Vengeance is mine!" She entered Princess Grace's hallowed hall and trashed the place. She upended the half-full waste basket and pulled out all the clothing hanging in the closet piling them into a mound.

Just as Katie finished her sweet revenge, her Mom returned carrying a large bag. "Look, Katie, I got a coat for Grace so you can have your coat back . . ." Before Mom finished her sentence in walked Princess Grace.

"Hey Katie, I brought your coat back. I should've asked you first but I was in a huge hurry. I had an interview for a job – which, by the way, is why I didn't respond to your text. I was in the interview and then I just rushed over to return your coat and tell you, I got the job! Can't stay though, I just need something from my room," rambled Grace in what all seemed to be one long sentence. Mom followed Grace to her room showing her the coat she bought.

"Oh, Mom, it's perfect; I love it!" Grace said as she opened the door to her room.

There was a loud scream from Grace and then their mother yelled, "Katie, what on earth did you do?"

Use the passage on page 60 to answer the questions. Cite evidence from the text to support your responses.

1. What does the story tell you about Katie?

   _____

   _____

2. What can you infer about Katie?

   _____

   _____

3. What does the story tell you about Grace?

   _____

   _____

4. What can you infer about Grace?

   _____

   _____

5. What can you infer about the relationship between Katie and Grace?

   _____

   _____

6. What can you infer about how Katie's mom felt about Grace?

   _____

   _____

7. What do you think happened next?

   _____

   _____

   _____

Read the passage. Then, answer the questions on page 63.

# The Baseball Card

"I have to keep my hand from shaking," thought Mark as he picked up the baseball card. Suddenly, the air in the swap meet seemed too warm. He stared at the early twentieth-century image and then slowly turned the card over.

"That's one of my favorites," said the elderly man. "My dad got that in a pack of gum when he was a boy."

"How…how much?" asked Mark casually as he cleared his voice.

The man thought for a minute. "Fifty dollars," he said. Then he bit his lip. "Maybe it was too much to ask, especially from a boy," he thought.

Mark felt his head swimming. The baseball card was in perfect condition. It showed the open, friendly face of Honus Wagner, a player from the Pittsburgh Pirates. Wagner had played with the Pirates until the outbreak of World War I. Nearly 20 years later, he had been one of the first players inducted into the Baseball Hall of Fame. Mark looked at the old man and knew he did not realize what a treasure he had.

The man watched Mark as he studied the card. "I sure could use that fifty dollars," the man thought. He would settle for forty dollars, but he wanted to see what the boy would say first.

Mark looked at the man's face and the frayed collar of his shirt. "I've never seen him at one of these swap meets before," thought Mark. "I bet he is here because he needs some money, not because he knows a lot about baseball cards." Mark closed his eyes for a moment. "What do I do?" he asked himself. "If I made this trade, it would be the biggest thing that ever happened to me. But I would have to remember that I robbed this man for the rest of my life."

The man looked at the boy hopefully, and then his heart sank as Mark shook his head and handed back the card. "How will I pay for that prescription?" he wondered. "How 'bout forty dollars?" the man questioned, almost begged.

Mark hesitated for a minute, and then he leaned forward. "Look," he said. "I know a lot about baseball cards. You should not be selling this card here. You need to take it to an antiques dealer." The man's eyes widened as Mark added, "That card is worth a lot more than $50. The last time a Honus Wagner card was sold, it made more than half a million dollars." Then he turned and walked away, before the old man could see the tears in Mark's eyes. Walking away was the hardest thing Mark had ever done in his life.

Use the passage on page 62 to answer the questions. Cite evidence from the passage to support your responses.

1. From what point of view is "The Baseball Card" written?

   _____

   _____

2. Is this point of view omniscient or limited?

   _____

   _____

3. What is the first clue in the story that the baseball card is valuable?

   _____

   _____

4. What is the old man's worry about Mark?

   _____

   _____

5. Describe Mark as a character. What are his main characteristics?

   _____

   _____

6. Describe the old man as a character. What are his main characteristics?

   _____

   _____

7. How would this story be different if you were unable to read the thoughts of the characters? What information would be missing?

   _____

   _____

   _____

Read the story. Then, answer the questions on page 65.

# Hide-and-Seek

As Bill started to count, Avery scooted off as fast as his six-year-old legs could carry him. He was excited; Bill had agreed to play hide-and-seek with him! Since Bill entered middle school, he seemed to have outgrown childish games, but Avery craved Bill's attention. Bill was Avery's hero, so it really stung the day Avery overheard Bill talking to their mom when she had asked Bill to play a game with Avery, "Aw, Mom, he is such a baby. Seriously it is not fun to play with him because he is not a challenge."

Avery was determined to show Bill that he was a challenge and worthy of his time for games.

Bill counted slowly and loudly so that Avery could hear him better. When he reached 25, he stopped.

"Hmm! I wonder where he could be," Bill exclaimed in a playful, wise older-sibling voice.

"Is he in here?" Bill queried as he opened the door to Avery's junk-laden, clothing-strewn, chaotic closet. "No."

"Well, that was strange," Bill thought. "Avery always began the hide-and-seek game by hiding in his closet."

Next Bill searched through his own bedroom, Dad and Mom's room, and the laundry area—especially the clothes dryer. Mom forbade that hideout, but with Avery you never knew. Nope. Only their mom was in the laundry room folding some clothes from the dryer.

"Hey, Mom, any idea where Avery's hiding?" There was just a touch of worry in Bill's question.

Mom gave a playful half-smile. "Hmm, seems like Avery is getting better at hiding."

"Yeah, I've looked around for more than ten minutes. I don't think Avery can keep this hiding stuff up much longer."

"Well I thought I heard the door open. Why don't you check outdoors?" Mom suggested.

"What? Ever since Dad told that scary story, Avery has been too afraid to go outside by himself," Bill replied in disbelief.

"That was a year ago, I think Avery has outgrown that. Besides, someone opened the door. Go and take a look!" urged Mom.

Bill chuckled to himself, "Avery outside? No way." Bill strolled off toward the play fort; but Avery wasn't there. He wasn't behind the garbage cans either. Then Bill heard a faint moaning. Bill walked to the side of the house where the noise was coming from, he saw the old maple tree, and looked up. A small boy sat with a red shirt and a redder face.

"Hey, Bill, can you help me get down from here?" Avery asked with his voice trembling.

## Hide-and-Seek (continued)

"Wow, good hiding place, kid. I didn't think you had it in you," Bill said in amazement as he clambered up the tree to help his brother.

Once the brothers were both down safely, Bill turned to Avery and said, "I'm impressed; you were a real challenge to find!"

Avery just beamed.

Use the story on page 64 to answer the questions. Cite evidence from the story to support your responses.

1.  From what point of view is this story written?

    A.  first person from Bill's perspective

    B.  first person from Avery's perspective

    C.  second person

    D.  third person

2.  What does Bill think about playing hide-and-seek with Avery?

    _____

    _____

3.  How does Bill's thinking change from the beginning of the story to the end?

    _____

    _____

    _____

4.  What does Avery think about playing hide-and-seek with Bill?

    _____

    _____

5.  How would this passage be different if it were told from a different point of view?

    _____

    _____

    _____

Read the article. Then, answer the questions on page 67.

# Ban Oxygen on Everest

Mount Everest is the world's highest mountain rising 29,035 feet (8,850 m) high. The great mountain has dared many a thrill-seeker to scale its fortress. Climbing Everest poses many challenges for mountaineers. The extreme terrain is steep and icy, the weather is extremely cold, and the lack of oxygen as the climbers reach such heights are all factors that make the climb very dangerous.

For the first 74 years of climbing Mount Everest, 144 lives were lost—an average of about 2 lives a year. In a single climbing season in the late 1990s, 12 people perished in their attempts to climb Everest. The increasing commercialization of Everest can be blamed. Guides and Sherpas charge tens of thousands of dollars for their services. They haul climbers of questionable skills up and down the mountain.

In order to reduce the number of deaths, some suggest that oxygen canisters be banned from the summit, except for emergencies. Without supplemental oxygen, inexperienced and unprepared climbers would probably collapse at the lower, safer levels. With supplemental oxygen, they climb higher. Accomplished mountaineers in supreme physical condition would still be able to reach the summit. Less accomplished mountaineers would be forced to turn back at lower levels.

Another benefit of banning oxygen canisters would be for safety of rescuers. Those caught in storms or experiencing medical problems would be more accessible to help. If supplementary oxygen allows them to climb beyond their natural physical limits, rescuers lives are risked, too.

The ban of oxygen canisters would have another benefit from an ecological perspective. It would eliminate the scandalous littering of the world's most famous mountain. As climbers ascend up the mountain they discard the used oxygen canisters. It is also common practice to leave the bodies of the people who die on the climb on the mountain. The Sherpas refer to Everest as Mother Goddess of the Earth. Are used oxygen canisters and corpses of paying clients fitting ornaments for such a goddess to wear?

Use the passage on page 66 to answer the questions. Cite evidence from the text to support your responses.

1.  What is the author's purpose for writing this article?

    _____

    _____

    _____

2.  What is the author's point of view?

    _____

    _____

    _____

3.  How might this passage be different if it were written from the point of view of a Sherpa?

    _____

    _____

    _____

4.  Is this passage more fact-based or opinion-based?

    _____

    _____

5.  Does the author present enough evidence to support his claim? Explain.

    _____

    _____

    _____

6.  Write an example of the author's use of personification in this passage.

    _____

    _____

Match each quotation with the character trait listed.

# Character Quotes

1. _____ "Where are we? I thought this was . . . no, I guess not," stuttered Stephen.

2. _____ "I don't think I can walk another step," sighed Upton as he fell into a nearby recliner.

3. _____ "You can't make me finish my work," Sean shrieked as he stomped his foot.

4. _____ "Oops! Sorry. I thought you were my brother," moaned Sarah as she wiped ketchup off the waiter's white shirt.

5. _____ "Oh, cool. I've been looking for this baseball card for months!"

6. _____ "Oops! Sorry. I didn't mean to step on your foot. Oh, dear, I just did it again," said Gavin as he tripped over his own feet.

7. _____ "Would you like to go to the dance, I mean, if you wouldn't be embarrassed to go with me?"

8. _____ "Those kids are always coming in my yard chasing after their ball. They have no respect."

9. _____ "Please can I have a later curfew, just this once? I never get to stay out as late as my friends."

10. _____ "This place is a dump! Hey, loser, get over here and take my order."

11. _____ "Good evening, Mr. Ito, I brought you some soup to help you feel better."

12. _____ "I promise I will always stay with you through thick and thin."

A. exhausted

B. whiny

C. devoted

D. clumsy

E. stubborn

F. obnoxious

G. excited

H. insecure

I. grouchy

J. kind

K. confused

L. embarrassed

Read each character description and match it to its character stereotype.

# Characters on Campus

1. _____ She's beautiful and peppy. She can always be seen with a smile on her face. Some people think that she is superficial and fake.

A. football player

2. _____ He is a wisecracker always ready with a humorous observation or a quick comeback.

B. scholar

C. class clown

3. _____ She's beautiful and full of energy.  She is always seen listening to music. People are amazed at her flexibility and coordination.

D. cheerleader

E. captain of the debate team

4. _____ He towers over everyone else and has an amazing jump shot.

F. president of the science club

5. _____ He is already thinking about which Ivy League school he will attend for college. He may be smart, but he is socially awkward.

G. captain of the dance team

H. basketball player

6. _____ She always has her nose in a book. Her favorite pastime is memorizing the periodic table.

7. _____ He is a big man on campus, but not just because he is tall. As the quarterback, he seems to get all the girls.

8. _____ He is a talker—always has something to add or another way to look at any perspective.

9. All of the above characterizations are exaggerated stereotypes. Choose one of the characters and write a more realistic, complex description.

_____

_____

_____

Read the passage. Then, answer the questions on page 71.

# In Another Country

Wesley King and his family lived in Central America. Both of his parents were teachers in an English-speaking school. Wesley learned Spanish and made friends with many of the students at the school. The experience of being in another country was great. However, Wesley felt troubled for much of the two years he had lived there.

Much of what troubled Wesley was due to the economic hardships he observed in Central America. In most of the city in which he lived, the people were poor. Some of their homes were made from mud and bricks, while others lived in shacks of corrugated metal. Wesley saw the children from these homes walking back and forth from the community well all day, carrying water to their homes because they had no plumbing.

Before Wesley and his parents had moved to their Central American home, they had attended classes called "orientation workshops." They were told that the city they were moving to had many beggars. The orientation trainer warned them not to give the beggars money. "It doesn't teach these people how to be constructive members of society," she said. "And the beggars never learn how to be self-sufficient without charity. Sometimes they force their children to beg and they grow up knowing nothing else."

Still, Wesley wanted to do something to help the people who were less fortunate than he was. There was a little girl in a blue dress who sold flowers with her blind grandmother. The girl was only about six years old, and she seemed frail, even though she always smiled. Wesley bought flowers from them often and brought the flowers home to give to his mother and sisters.

Wesley was most aware of the poverty in Central America when he and his parents would go out to eat in restaurants. Beggars would line up outside the restaurant, looking for leftover food from sympathetic diners. After seeing this, Wesley decided he could help by volunteering at a local food kitchen. It operated out of a church that was between his school and his house. The kitchen provided food and found employment opportunities for poor people.

Yesterday, Wesley learned that his parents have teaching jobs in the United States for the next school year. In a few short months, his family will be returning to their old home in Connecticut. Wesley is excited about seeing his grandparents and going to school again with his cousins. He knows he will miss the friends he made at the food kitchen, but he plans to make new friends at a volunteer food bank for poor people in Connecticut.

Use the passage on page 70 to answer the questions. Cite evidence from the passage to support your responses.

1. Choose three words or phrases to describe Wesley.

   _____

   _____

2. What is Wesley's main concern since he has lived in Central America?

   _____

   _____

   _____

3. Do you think Wesley agreed or disagreed with the trainer in his orientation workshops?

   _____

   _____

   _____

4. What does Wesley see when he goes out to eat with his family?

   _____

   _____

   _____

5. What suggestions would you make to help Wesley with his concerns?

   _____

   _____

   _____

   _____

Read the letter. Then, complete the character web on page 73.

# The Dinner Party

Cleveland, Ohio
July 12, 1880

My Dear Grace,

Last night, Arthur and I had the honor of attending a dinner at the Rockefellers' home on Euclid Avenue. The common people of the town call this street "Millionaires' Row," and I must say the many mansions are impressive. But, I admit that Mr. Rockefeller surprised me. Unlike other nabobs who go overboard to impress guests with their wealth, the celebrated John D. seems to be a genuinely simple man. A friend of mine told me that one of his favorite meals is bread and milk. Can you imagine that, Grace? This is a man who can afford any delicacy in the world, and he prefers bread and milk!

You and I have both heard the stories of the ruthless ways in which this man acquired his wealth, but after meeting him, I am skeptical. He was down-to-earth and amusing. I truly enjoyed meeting him.

Mr. Rockefeller talked to me during the soup course about his mother, speaking quite movingly about her religious faith and his admiration of the way she brought him up. Once, John and his brothers went skating on a frozen river, knowing full well that their mother had forbidden this and they would be punished if they were caught. While they were on the river, they saved the life of a boy who had fallen through the ice. Not bending an inch from her rules, their mother still punished them for their disobedience—although she did praise them for their heroic action first. He also told me that he made his first money raising turkeys, saving every penny after he sold the birds.

Later in the meal, one man who undoubtedly was trying to impress our host began a financial discussion that bored most of the guests to death. Our host, the richest man in the world, picked up a cracker and proceeded to balance it on the end of his nose! He grinned widely when he managed this trick on his first attempt. Everyone broke into laughter and applause.

The meal was excellent, but not lavish; so were the surroundings. The simplicity of the entertainment and the dinner was unexpected, but even more so was the simplicity and modesty of our host.

Please give my regards to all. I hope this letter finds you well, my dear friend. I will be home soon and will tell you more then.

Yours ever,
Irene

Name_____

Complete the character web using evidence from the letter on page 72 to support your responses.

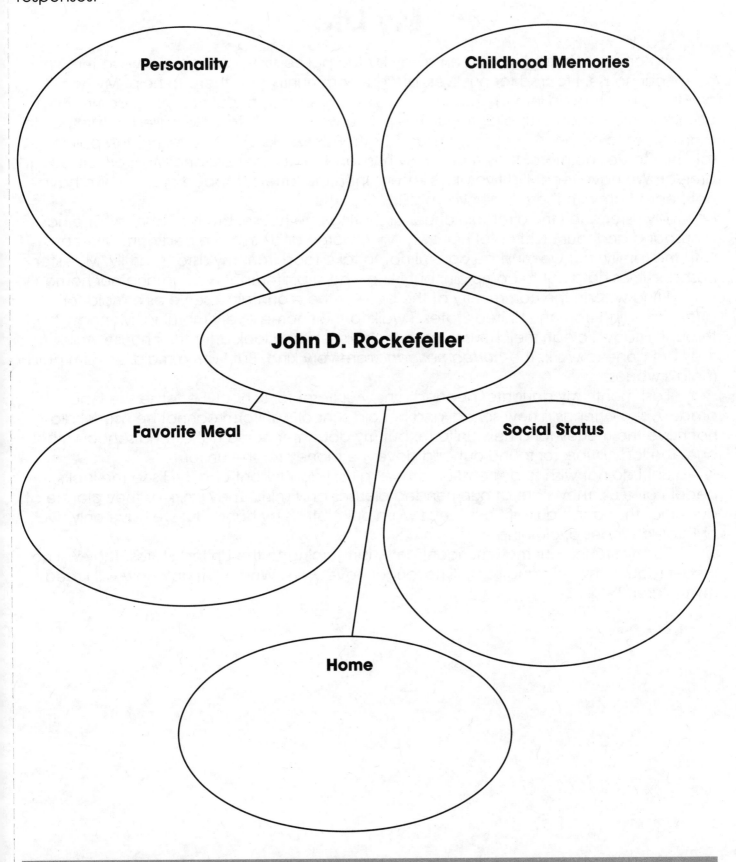

Personality

Childhood Memories

John D. Rockefeller

Favorite Meal

Social Status

Home

Read the narrative. Then, answer the questions on page 75.

# My Life

When my husband was taken away by the police six years ago, we were thrown out of our house. I feared for our lives, but our community was there to help. My two children and I moved into the home of my sister. Friends from our mountain community gathered clothes and supplies for us. The padre was a dear, too. He called on the police many times to gather news of my husband. After six weeks of his pestering, the police told him to call no more. They moved my husband to another province to work on a road project. We have received five of his letters, then the letters stopped coming. We have not heard from him these past two years.

My sister and I try to remain cheerful sharing one house, but it's not easy. She has a husband and four children of her own. My children and I share a bedroom. We eat with the family, but we must be careful not to take food from my sister's family. My sister's husband tries hard not to complain, but I know he'd prefer that we find another home.

I find work in the community at the base of the mountain. I serve as a maid for a family visiting from the United States. I walk to their home every morning, Monday through Friday. I clean their house, wash their dishes, and look after their house while they are gone to work. The *norteamericanos* are very kind. But I am a maid, so I am paid maid's wages.

Last month my daughter needed a new uniform for school. Because she is now in grade 7, she attends a new school and her old school's uniform cannot be used. I did not have the money for a new uniform, but my daughter could not attend school without one. The lady I work for found out and gave me money for the uniform.

But I do not wish to depend on others' gifts. I don't want charity. I see the looks people give us. They stare at our mended blouses and shirts. They smirk as they glance at our shoes that don't quite fit our feet. I wash our clothes by hand. But we have only two or three changes of clothing.

Today I found out my American family is returning to the United States. They will no longer require my help and so I will no longer have work. What will I do? How will I feed my children?

Read the personal narrative on page 74. Then, complete the page.

1. Write 3 words that describe the author of the narrative.

   _____     _____     _____

2. Order the author's concerns from **1–6**, 1 being the most and 6 the least. Explain your reasoning.

   _____ food          _____ work          _____ husband

   _____ pride         _____ children      _____ clothes

   _____

   _____

   _____

   _____

3. Write a paragraph using the words in question 1 to describe the author of the narrative. Cite evidence from the text to support your response.

   _____

   _____

   _____

   _____

   _____

   _____

   _____

   _____

4. On a separate sheet of paper or on the computer, write a personal narrative about your life and how your needs for food and clothing are met.

Read the passage. Then, answer the questions on page 77.

# Just Friends

Jake awkwardly kicked at a clump of weeds along the sidewalk outside King Middle School. He missed the after-school bus again and was trying to decide what to do. He couldn't call home because his mom had an important meeting at work this afternoon and his dad was out of town on business all week. No way would he call Jill. She'd still be in class anyway, but he knew better than to ask his sister for a ride. She didn't have time in her busy life for such mundane errands as picking up her younger brother from school. He figured it would be best to walk home—might even be good for him—and it really wasn't that bad of a walk, just a little over a mile.

As Jake walked home he thought about the real reason he missed the bus, Jenna Lee. Every Thursday she had a viola lesson after school in the music room which just happened to be next to Jake's locker. Every Thursday Jake stalled at his locker rearranging his books and jamming a couple of papers into his pack. Every Thursday Jenna would stop to talk with Jake about nothing in particular. She had the most beautiful eyes and the best smile and her voice was a musical, tingling voice and she had a great sense of humor . . . Jake went into his usual trance extolling her virtues both physically and personality-wise.

But today it was more; they really talked—about Logan's party coming up next week, about the boring history project, about Mr. Hansen's mismatched socks, about all the important stuff of eighth grade. Yep, definitely worth missing the bus and having to walk home for, he thought to himself.

But he and Jenna were just friends; he wasn't about to get goofy over some girl. He had too much to worry about with football and grades and well, other stuff; but maybe they'd hang out at Logan's party. Jenna seemed glad to hear he was going; yea, friends hang out at parties. And maybe he'd text her later tonight, like friends. Jake smiled to himself as he drifted off into the text conversation he and Jenna might have.

Honk! The loud yet familiar noise brought Jake back from his daydream to the present moment. "Where are you going?" Jill asked as she rolled down her window and pulled up beside her brother. "You walked right past our house, you know?"

"Just trying to get some extra exercise to keep in shape for football," he said confidently trying to cover for his mistake. "I'm glad Jenna and I are just friends," he laughed to himself.

Use the passage on page 76 to answer the questions. Cite evidence from the text to support your responses.

1.   Choose two words to describe Jake.

_____

_____

2.   Choose two words to describe Jenna.

_____

_____

3.   Choose two words to describe Jill.

_____

_____

4.   Do you think Jake and Jill will continue to be "just friends"? Explain.

_____

_____

5.   Write a dialogue that Jake and Jenna may have had after school that day.

_____

_____

_____

_____

_____

_____

_____

_____

Read the passage. Then, complete the graphic organizer on page 79.

# In an Incan Village

Imagine if you will, an Incan farming village in the 1400s at the height of their civilization. Picture the Andes, huge, snow-capped mountains towering over a small cluster of huts. The small, brown, grass-roofed huts in the village are made out of dried, mud called *adobe*. Against the steep slopes of the mountains, crops grow on terraces watered by canals dug around the mountains moving water from the mountains to water the crops.

The sleeping village wakes early, when the air flowing down the mountains is still cold and blusters between the huts. Children go out to gather sticks to feed the fire, but there are few trees, so hunting for sticks is a challenge. The rough barking of dogs and the rumbling bray of llamas can be heard in every hut. After a small meal, some villagers take their goats and sheep out to graze, while others go to work in the fields.

At midday, the main meal is prepared. A strong, bitter scent drifts from the clay jugs of chichi, a drink made from corn. It mixes with the spicy scent of guinea-pig stew cooking over the fire. Dried herbs and chilies are added to the stew as it cooks. As the sun reaches down to the little village, heavy woolen blankets as rough as dry grass are spread over stools or fences to dry and air out. Excitement spreads through the village at the sight of *chasqui*, a messenger, who is carrying news and information from the cities to the smaller villages. Most of the villagers gather to hear what this visitor has to say.

In the evening, the distant cries of birds echo in the mountains. The last light illuminates the highest point in the village, kept for religious ceremonies because it is closest to the sun. As the light dies, the fires burn to red-gold embers and the people of the village go, one by one, to sleep.

When the Spanish explorers came to this area in Peru, they forced the Incas off the land and destroyed the farms. Only remnants of these ancient villages and their farms remained. However, these remnants provided for archaeologists a clue into the life and culture of this community. In 1977, a project was formed to rebuild the farms and irrigation systems that once existed along the base of the Andes so that local families could once again grow their crops.

Use the passage on page 78 to complete the graphic organizer to describe parts of the passage. Cite evidence from the passage to support your descriptions. Tell what sense was invoked by the description used.

| Object | Description | Sense |
|---|---|---|
| 1.  huts | | |
| 2.  mountains | | |
| 3.  air | | |
| 4.  animals | | |
| 5.  blankets | | |
| 6.  stew | | |
| 7.  fields | | |
| 8.  chichi | | |
| 9.  birds | | |
| 10.  fire | | |

11.  Write a description of your room, using all five senses.

_____

_____

_____

_____

_____

_____

_____

Read the passage. Then, complete the activities on page 81.

# London in 1601

This city being very large of itself, has very **extensive** suburbs, and a fort called the Tower, of beautiful structure. (The city) is magnificently **ornamented** with public buildings and churches, of which there are above one hundred and twenty.

On the south is a bridge (London Bridge) of stone 883 feet (269 m) in length, of wonderful work; it is supported upon twenty piers of square stone, sixty feet high and thirty broad, joined by arches of about twenty feet diameter. The whole is covered on each side with houses so **disposed** as to have the appearance of a continued street, not at all of a bridge. Upon this is built a tower, on whose top the heads of such as have been executed for high treason are placed on iron spikes: we counted above thirty.

Paulus Jovius, in his description of the most remarkable towns in England, says all are **obscured** by London… its houses are elegantly built, its churches fine, its towns strong, and its riches and abundance surprising. The wealth of the world is **wafted** to it by the Thames, swelled by the tide, and navigable to merchant ships through a safe and deep channel for sixty miles, from its mouth to the city. Its banks are everywhere beautified with fine country seats, woods, and farms; below is the royal palace of Greenwich; above, that of Richmond; and between both, on the west of London, rise the noble buildings of Westminster, most remarkable for the courts of justice, the parliament, and St. Peter's Church, enriched with the royal tombs.

This river abounds in swans, swimming in flocks: the sight of them, and their noise, are vastly agreeable to the fleets that meet them in their course. It is joined to the city by a bridge of stone, wonderfully built; is never increased by any rains, rising only with the tide, and is everywhere spread with nets for taking salmon and **shad**.

Excerpted from *Fragment Regalia* by Sir Robert Naunton

Use the passage on page 80 to complete the activities.

1. Write a description of each of the setting details from the passage.

London Bridge: _____

_____

the towns: _____

_____

Thames River: _____

_____

Westminster: _____

_____

2. Define each word as it is used in the passage. Use context clues and a dictionary as necessary.

extensive: _____

ornamented: _____

disposed: _____

obscured: _____

wafted: _____

shad: _____

3. Use the Internet to research what London is like today. Write a descriptive paragraph on a separate sheet of paper or the computer, describing the city. Then, write a second paragraph describing how the city has or has not changed in over 400 years.

Read the passage. Then, complete the activities on page 83.

# In the Still of the Night

Even though the night was warm, Keisha was shaking like a leaf as she slipped softly out of her sleeping bag. Quietly, stealthily, she made her way down the narrow path to the twins' tent. The twigs and pine needles crackled under her bare feet.

"Arianna! Quiana! Wake up!" she hissed. "Let me in. It's Keisha!"

As fast as two bleary-eyed, half-asleep kids can, Arianna and Quiana obliged. The three girls were seated cross-legged in the cramped little tent.

"What's up, Keisha? You act like you've seen Big Foot," giggled Arianna.

Keisha shuddered and shook unable to quiet the emotional chaos within her. Sensing that their friend was serious, both Quiana and Arianna scooted closer to Keisha to comfort her.

"What is it?" began Arianna.

"And where's Tristan?" continued Quiana.

"That's just it!" wailed Keisha. "She's missing. I just woke up a few minutes ago and her sleeping bag was empty...and she was gone. I think something awful has happened!"

"Now you're scaring us," wailed Arianna and Quiana at the same time and a little too loudly.

"Shh! Keep quiet. Whatever or whoever got Tristan may still be around," warned Keisha in a whisper.

Outside the tent they heard the sound of something thrashing about in the bushes. The three girls looked at one another.

"What are we going to do?" mouthed Quiana without making a sound, and flapping her hands.

"We've got to help Tristan," whispered Keisha taking charge. "Come on, together on three. One...Two...Three!"

Screaming like howler monkeys, the three campers poured out of the tent. They continued to scream as they clamored in the direction of the thrashing sound.

"We've got you, you...you...beast!" snarled Quiana in her fiercest voice.

"Quiana? Arianna? Keisha? Is that you?" It was Tristan. She stumbled toward them looking a little embarrassed. She explained how she struggles with somnambulant behavior or sleepwalking. Apparently in her sleep, she had opened a jar of raspberry jam and ate some. When a noise startled her she woke up and was embarrassed at the mess she had made of herself, so she went to wash off in the river a few yards away. The girls all started to laugh until the twins' dad, who was in the tent a few feet away, yelled at them to quiet down and get back in their tents.

Name_____

Use the passage on page 82 to complete the activities.

1. Complete the chart with information about the setting.

| | |
|---|---|
| Location | |
| Time of Day | |
| Time of the Year | |
| Real or Imaginary | |

2. What is the conflict in the story?

_____

3. How does the setting of the story add to the conflict of the story?

_____

_____

4. Who are the characters in the story?

_____

5. How does the setting of the story help the reader better understand the characters?

_____

_____

_____

6. On a separate sheet of paper or on the computer, rewrite this story placing the characters in another setting.

Read the passage. Then, answer the questions on page 85.

# Dad's Favorite Place

David's dad was going to go bowling tonight, just like he had every Thursday night for as long as David could remember. He did so for relaxation he said, although David couldn't understand how rolling a heavy ball into pins with the hope of creating a crashing noise could be relaxing. Relaxing for David was curling up with a good book, but he still wished his dad would take him to the bowling alley with him.

"Hey, Dad, can I go bowling with you tonight?" David pleaded for the hundredth Thursday night in a row.

Mom frowned. "David, Dad works hard and deserves a night out with his friends," Mom repeated for the hundredth Thursday night in a row. David knew his dad worked hard—it showed in his tired eyes and haggard body—but David craved time with his dad so he continued to ask hoping that one Thursday night the answer might change.

Dad smiled at David. "So, you'd like to go bowling with me, huh? Well, my friends did back out on me tonight. I guess I could use some company. There's only one problem," his dad continued, "If I take you, I'll have to take your older brother and sister, too."

David hadn't considered Ben and Tara; it was a good thing his dad had! If his dad had taken him but left them home, they would have been really ticked and would have made life miserable for him for days.

So as Dad went out to warm up the old Chevy pickup, David gathered Ben and Tara. They all piled in the cab scrunched in close and headed to the bowling alley— Dad's special place!

As they entered the old brick building, David was overwhelmed with the smoke smell that permeated the air, but then he caught sight of the bright lights displaying the scores and heard the loud sound of crashing pins being laid to rest. They were in Dad's haven and it was perfect. Dad rented shoes and balls for each of the kids and then put on his own special pair of shoes and polished his special ball that he pulled from his own bag.

Dad showed the kids how to hold the heavy ball, stand, aim, step forward, swing back the arm, and releasing the ball forward toward the pins. When Dad went effortlessly through the steps, his ball went straight down the alley, knocking all ten pins with a loud crash! When David, Ben, and Tara attempted to execute the steps, the ball slowly made its way down the alley in a pace that was difficult to endure, kind of like watching a pot of water boil. More often than not the ball would find its way to the gutter before reaching the pins—gutter ball—a new term David became very familiar with. But no matter how poorly the kids bowled, Dad beamed. He enjoyed spending time doing what he enjoyed most with the people he enjoyed most—and they enjoyed spending time with Dad.

Use the passage on page 84 to answer the questions. Cite evidence from the text to support your responses.

1.  The setting of this story changes three times. List each setting and describe it.

    _____

    _____

    _____

2.  Choose one of the settings and write three or four sentences describing it in more detail as you imagine it.

    _____

    _____

    _____

    _____

3.  How do you think David feels about his dad?

    _____

    _____

4.  Write about a special place you like to spend time with a special adult in your life. Be sure to describe the place using your senses and descriptive words.

    _____

    _____

    _____

    _____

    _____

    _____

    _____

Read the passage. Then, answer the questions on page 87.

# The Key Clue

The day started like any other day at Lincoln Middle School; until the announcement came over the intercom.

"Sorry for this interruption, but we have experienced a crime on our campus today," Mr. Rivera, the principal, explained. "A car in our visitors' parking lot was keyed. We will not tolerate this kind of vandalism and will be working hard to find the person who did this. If you have any information regarding this incident, please come to the office during the passing period. Thank you."

During the passing period two students claimed to have witnessed the incident, and each cast suspicion on the other. Principal Rivera called each student individually and listened closely to their stories. First, he called in Mason.

"I got to school late—I couldn't find my math homework and if I missed another homework assignment I would get detention—so I didn't see it happen—the keying, I mean; but I did see Matt—at least I think it was Matt—it was a dark-haired kid wearing a red T-shirt. Anyway, I saw this kid cutting between two cars in the visitors' parking lot. I thought it was weird, because kids aren't usually in the visitors' parking lot especially in the morning. Then he almost bumped into me as he ran passed the office. I was going into the office to get a tardy slip. Again, I didn't see who it was because I was digging in my backpack for the note my mother wrote for me to give to the attendance clerk. But I think it was Matt. But like I said, I'm not sure because I was a little preoccupied with my own issues."

Mr. Rivera thanked Mason for his statement and sent him back to class. He called Matt into his office.

"He's lying," Matt blurted out. "He probably blamed me; but I didn't do it. He probably said he saw someone with my description; but it's Spirit Day, and everyone is wearing red T-shirts. I think it was him. He was late to class and hurrying into the office and was mumbling something about how he was worried about getting in trouble. I think he keyed the car and then went to the office for a tardy slip. Besides I was in my first period class. You can ask Ms. Valdez. I left the room for a minute to use the bathroom, but that is it. Honest."

Mr. Rivera looked at Matt and said, "You want to try your story again? Your facts aren't adding up. I think you are the guilty one."

Name_____

Use the passage on page 86 to answer the questions. Cite evidence from the story to support your responses.

1. What is the setting of the story?

   _____

2. Who are the characters in the story? Give a brief description of each character.

   _____

   _____

   _____

3. What is the conflict of the story?

   _____

   _____

4. What is the building action in the story?

   _____

   _____

5. What is the turning point of the story?

   _____

   _____

6. What genre is this story?_____

7. What clues helped Mr. Rivera determine that it was Matt who keyed the car?

   _____

   _____

8. Did Mr. Rivera have enough evidence to prove who keyed the car? Explain.

   _____

   _____

   _____

Read the passage. Then, answer the questions on page 89.

# High-Tech Tale

It was the summer of 2020. I was 15 years old, and a computer changed my life. Up until that summer, I had used the computer just like everyone else my age: to link with my instructors, to find film clips and original documents for research, to play the occasional game, and to keep in touch with my friends around the world. But suddenly, I realized the computer was a magic carpet, a door into any world I wanted to explore. I spent hour after hour on the Internet, going on virtual tours of cities, national parks, and amusement parks. I started emailing more and more people and spent whole days keeping up with my correspondence. "Jan, did you ever eat lunch?" my mother would ask. "Have you been outside today? Did you take the garbage out like I asked?" Of course, the answer was always no. I hadn't done anything except sit at my computer. I was engrossed by the wealth of information and adventures to be had through its screen.

Then things went from bad to worse. My friend Jeremy and I took the high-speed train downtown to the library. When we missed our stop we ended up two cities away. We decided to take a walk before catching the train back. Around a dark corner under the elevated train tracks, we saw a dingy storefront. It featured a virtual-reality smorgasbord of computer gear and video games. "Come in, come in," said the wraith-like store clerk, who was dressed in floating silk robes. Her voice was silken, too, and hypnotic. Before I knew what I was doing, I had purchased a game called *Mystic Manipulator*. I tucked the package under my arm and we caught the train home.

Within days, I was addicted to my new game, a virtual-reality fantasy. My part was as a shapeshifter in a band of adventurers. I could become any creature imaginable, and I was always the hero in every perilous situation that we encountered. The characters in the game became more real to me than my own friends. In fact, I began refusing calls and emails from my friends, and I never went to family meals. I stayed up most of the night because each adventure on *Mystic Manipulator* was more exciting than the last. I didn't want to miss anything.

After a week, my parents burst into my room with an Internet officer, who unplugged my computer right in the middle of a game. I howled with rage as I was taken off to the Center for Online Addiction. But I needed help. I had lost 20 pounds and was suffering from both malnutrition and sleep deprivation. I hadn't bathed in days, my hair was falling out, and I was weak and dizzy. I was put in the hospital wing of the center. Meanwhile, my mother and father packed up my computer and sent it to an elementary school. They also reported the woman who had sold me *Mystic Manipulator* for selling dangerous software to minors. By the end of the summer, I was much better, but was forbidden any computer use for six months. Instead, I was given an antique machine called a typewriter to use for reports and papers.

Use the passage on page 88 to answer the questions.

1. What is the conflict in *High-Tech Tale*?

   A. Jan doesn't want to return to school.

   B. Jan becomes too involved in her research.

   C. Jan spends an unhealthy amount of time on her computer.

   D. Jan and her friend become lost in a strange city.

2. What are the first signs that Jan is spending too much time on her computer?

   A. She emails more people and forgets to eat meals.

   B. She buys computer games and spends all her time playing them.

   C. She spends all of her time in chat rooms.

   D. She spends all of her time writing stories and posting them on the Internet.

3. When does Jan's situation get worse?

   A. when she buys new software to create stories and reports

   B. when she buys new software for a virtual-reality game

   C. when she and her friend Jeremy miss their train

   D. when she loses weight and becomes dehydrated

4. How is the conflict in the story resolved?

   A. when Jan's parents bring in an officer to unplug her computer

   B. when Jan throws away her game software

   C. when Jan starts emailing her real friends again

   D. when Jan's friend Jeremy talks to her and gets her help

5. What is one detail that shows this story is set in the future?

   A. computer games

   B. an Internet officer

   C. email to friends

   D. classes taken on the computer

6. What kind of help is Jan given?

   A. hospitalization and the removal of her computer

   B. a new diet and the removal of her game software

   C. starting school early and the removal of her computer

   D. going to stay with a different family

Read the passage. Then, answer the questions on page 91.

# When the Chips Are Down

It fell off again.

"This just won't work, Demetri," Sean said. "The pins are too loose on the chip."

"Maybe we can repair it. We sure can't afford a new chip like that one," replied Demetri.

Demetri's garage felt cooler than the sultry weather outside. The closed-in air held none of the Indian summer heat that would creep under the door or force itself through the thin glass of the window. It was too hot to work. Still, there was only a week and a half before the science fair. The heat was nothing compared to the drive the two students felt to win first place.

Sean tried to reconnect the pin to the computer chip. The soft metal solder slipped into the space near the pin. After it cooled, Sean urged the pins into the motherboard.

"Oh, no! It broke again. This just isn't going to work," growled Sean.

"What do you think we should do now?" questioned Demetri.

Sean simply shook his head. He knew that there was too little time to get enough money to buy the computer chip they needed to control the robot's "brain." Without that chip, it would be just like any other robot.

"Mom, would you be willing to lend Sean and me some money? We need it to finish our robot for the science fair," Demetri said to his mother as she fixed dinner.

"You know I would help if I could, but we just don't have the money right now. I'll be happy if I can pay the bills this month," his mother answered.

Demetri called Sean to tell him the bad news. The boys talked and became determined to earn money any way they could. Demetri washed cars for some people up the block. Sean cleaned at his father's shop after the workers left at night. Both boys babysat over the weekend, which they really hated. If it meant money for the computer chip, though, they were willing.

They had only two days to go until the science fair. Demetri and Sean slowly counted the money that they had worked so hard to earn. They had $62.30. It was a lot, but not enough for the chip. They were $18.70 short. It was time to tell their science teacher, Mrs. Foster.

"We tried, Mrs. Foster, but we just couldn't make enough money for the chip for our robot's brain," the students told her sadly.

Mrs. Foster smiled. "I have just the thing!" she said. She opened her desk drawer and took out a slip of paper. The boys were ecstatic when they saw it was a 25 percent off coupon for the local computer store.

When Sean and Demetri stood proudly next to their science fair exhibit, they had a robot that came to life.

Use the passage on page 90 to answer the questions. Cite evidence from the story to support your responses.

1. Who are the characters in this story? Describe each character.

   _____

   _____

   _____

2. What is the setting for the story?

   _____

   _____

   _____

3. What is the main conflict?

   _____

   _____

4. What is the rising action in the story?

   _____

   _____

5. What is the turning point in the story?

   _____

   _____

6. How is the conflict of the story resolved?

   _____

   _____

Read the passage. Then, answer the questions on page 93.

# Titania Arrives at the Bookshop

*Titania, a wealthy young woman whose father wants her to have the experience of working at a job, walks to the bookshop, where she meets her new employer, Roger Mifflin.*

Titania, after making sure that Edwards was out of sight, turned up Gissing Street with a fluent pace and an observant eye. A small boy cried, "Carry your bag, lady?" and she was about to agree, but then remembered that she was now engaged at ten dollars a week and waved him away.

Roger, who had conceived a notion of some rather peevish foundling of the Ritz-Carlton lobbies and Central Park riding academies, was agreeably amazed by the sweet simplicity of the young lady.

"Is this Mr. Mifflin?" she said, as he advanced all agog from his smoky corner.

"Miss Chapman?" he replied, taking her bag. "Helen!" he called. "Miss Titania is here."

She looked about the somber alcoves of the shop. "I do think it's adorable of you to take me in," she said. "Dad has told me so much about you. He says I'm impossible. I suppose this is the literature he talks about. I want to know all about it. And here's Bock!" she cried. "Dad says he's the greatest dog in the world, named after Botticelli or somebody. I've brought him a present. It's in my bag. Nice old Bocky!"

Bock, who was unaccustomed to spats, was examining them after his own fashion.

"Well, my dear," said Mrs. Mifflin. "We are delighted to see you. I hope you'll be happy with us, but I rather doubt it. Mr. Mifflin is a hard man to get along with."

"Oh, I'm sure of it!" cried Titania. "I mean, I'm sure I shall be happy! You mustn't believe a word of what Dad says about me. I'm crazy about books. I don't see how you can bear to sell them. I brought these violets for you, Mrs. Mifflin."

"How perfectly sweet of you," said Helen, captivated already. "Come along, we'll put them right in water. I'll show you your room."

"Before we begin," said Titania, "just let me give Bock his present." She showed a large package of tissue paper and, unwinding innumerable layers, finally disclosed a stalwart bone. "I was lunching at Sherry's, and I made the head waiter give this to me. He was awfully amused."

"Come along into the kitchen and give it to him," said Helen. "He'll be your friend for life."

Excerpted from *The Haunted Bookshop* by Christopher Morley (Melville House, 2013)

Use the passage on page 92 to answer the questions. Cite evidence from the passage to support your responses.

1. Who are the characters in this passage? Describe each character.

   _____

   _____

   _____

   _____

2. What is the setting of the passage?

   _____

   _____

3. What is the main conflict in the passage?

   _____

   _____

4. What is the rising action in the passage?

   _____

   _____

5. What is the turning point in the passage?

   _____

   _____

6. What is the falling action in the passage?

   _____

   _____

7. How is the conflict in this passage resolved?

   _____

   _____

# Nursery Headlines

Match the lines of the nursery rhymes and tunes to the headlines. Use a dictionary if needed.

Headlines

A. Two Dozen Fowl Baked in a Pastry

B. Young Shepherd Found Napping in Heap of Straw

C. Horseman Mistakes a Plume for Pasta

D. Rodent Scrambles Up Time Piece

E. Cantankerous Horticulturist Asked for Tips

F. Mother Comforts Child with a Thrasher

G. Track Star Warms Up with Taper

H. Young Mutton Follows Girl Closely

I. Diminutive Girl Loses Mutton

J. Jolly Ruler Requests His Delights

Nursery Rhymes and Tunes

_____ 1. Yankee Doodle went to town riding on his pony, stuck a feather in his hat and called it macaroni.

_____ 2. Hickory Dickory Dock, the mouse ran up the clock.

_____ 3. Hush little baby, don't say a word. Mama's going to buy you a mockingbird.

_____ 4. Mary had a little lamb; its fleece was white as snow and everywhere that Mary went the lamb was sure to go.

_____ 5. Jack be nimble, Jack be quick. Jack jumped over the candlestick.

_____ 6. Sing a song of sixpence a pocket full of rye. Four and twenty blackbirds baked in a pie.

_____ 7. Mary, Mary, quite contrary, how does your garden grow?

_____ 8. Where's the little boy who looks after the sheep? He's under the haystack fast asleep.

_____ 9. Little Bo Peep has lost her sheep and doesn't know where to find them.

_____ 10. Old King Cole was a merry old soul, and a merry old soul was he. He called for his pipe and he called for his bowl and he called for his fiddlers three.

Read each sentence. Draw a picture illustrating the literal meaning of each idiom. Then, write the idioms actual meaning.

# Literally Speaking

1. **Time flies** when I'm engrossed in a good book.

| Literal Meaning | Actual Meaning |
|---|---|
| | _____ |
| | _____ |
| | _____ |

2. Ben was **all ears** when his great-grandfather told stories about the war.

| Literal Meaning | Actual Meaning |
|---|---|
| | _____ |
| | _____ |
| | _____ |

3. Iman **hit the nail on the head** when he said that the coach was trying to relive his middle-school days.

| Literal Meaning | Actual Meaning |
|---|---|
| | _____ |
| | _____ |
| | _____ |

4. On a separate sheet of paper, make a list of 10 more idioms. Write the idioms in sentences. Draw the literal meanings, and then write the actual meanings.

Choose a word from the word bank that fits the description in column 1. Then, write your own related word in column 3.

# It's All Related

| Atlantic Ocean | bottle | Elvis | email |
|---|---|---|---|
| Henry Ford | historical fiction | linen | Miami |
| novel | pyramid | rock and roll | yard |

| Description | Word Bank Word | Your Word |
|---|---|---|
| 1.  inventor | | |
| 2.  fabric | | |
| 3.  city | | |
| 4.  communication tool | | |
| 5.  Egyptian structure | | |
| 6.  literature genre | | |
| 7.  container | | |
| 8.  body of water | | |
| 9.  musical genre | | |
| 10.  famous singer | | |
| 11.  something you read | | |
| 12.  standard measure | | |

Complete each sentence with a word from the word bank. Add a suffix if necessary for the word to fit the sentence. Use a dictionary if needed.

# Pros and Cons

| | | |
|---|---|---|
| conclude | conduct | congest |
| conjure | consult | contort |
| converge | proclaim | procrastinate |
| profit | prostrate | protest |
| provoke | proximate | |

1. Julio's face _____ in pain when his horse stepped on his foot.

2. Joanna's cold cause her sinuses to be _____.

3. The guilty child _____ up quite a lie to protect himself from being punished.

4. The man lay _____ after falling and bumping his head.

5. The _____ carried signs outside the White House gates.

6. His _____ was unbecoming of the office he held.

7. Jasper's _____ sibling was his brother Rudy who was only 10 months older.

8. Because Heather _____ in starting her report, she had to stay up very late to finish it.

9. Luke _____ his opinions even when no one wanted to hear them.

10. My dad _____ with another doctor before agreeing to the surgery.

11. The speaker _____ his speech with a story that brought all his points together.

12. The roads all _____ in the middle of the town square.

13. My sister has a way of _____ me to anger in the way no one else can.

Follow the directions to solve the riddle. Then, write a synonym for each bolded word on the line. Use a dictionary or thesaurus if needed.

# What Is It?

The person who built it doesn't want it. The person who bought it doesn't need it. The person who needs it doesn't know it. What is it?

___ ___ ___ ___ ___ ___ ___
(1)    (2)    (3)    (4)    (5)    (6)    (7)

1.   If a soldier is **valiant**, write **A** on line 1. If not, then write **I**.

_____

2.   If most fans think a football game **tedious**, write a **D** on line 2. If not, then write **C**.

_____

3.   If a **vial** can hold liquid, write **O** on line 3. If not, then write **E**.

_____

4.   If a 40-pound weakling has **brawn**, write **T** on line 4. If not, then write **F**.

_____

5.   If you can count to **infinity**, write **G** on line 5. If not, then write **F**.

_____

6.   If you should be **wary** of a friend request from a stranger, write **I** on line 6. If not, then write **E**.

_____

7.   If a person might feel **ardent** at the opening of their favorite play, write **N** on line 7. If not, then write **M**.

_____

Complete the proverbs with the words from the word bank. Then, write the meaning of the proverb.

# Proverbial Wisdom

| | | | |
|---|---|---|---|
| actions | bite | boils | broth |
| cooks | do | eggs | hand |
| island | man | omelet | pen |
| pot | Romans | sword | words |

1. The _____ is mightier than the _____.

   _____

2. When in Rome, _____ as the _____.

   _____

3. No _____ is an _____.

   _____

4. You can't make an _____ without breaking a few

   _____.

   _____

5. A watched _____ never _____.

   _____

6. _____ speak louder than _____.

   _____

7. Too many _____ spoil the _____.

   _____

8. Don't _____ the _____ that feed you.

   _____

Read the passage. Then, complete the activity on page 101.

# The Good Bacteria

What do you get if you mix **common** bacteria and vinegar? This is not the beginning of a joke. It is a serious scientific question. The answer is, you get bacteria that eat toxic **waste** and turn that waste into salt.

Bacteria can make you sick, but not all **strains** of bacteria are harmful. Some bacteria benefit human beings. Scientists have proposed a new, **beneficial** use for bacteria called bioremediation. Bioremediation uses specialized microorganisms for **toxic** cleanup. Vinegar **stimulates** these bacteria to consume the toxic liquids. The bacteria transform the toxins into salt. The bacteria **function** in closed-in places, without sunlight, and they produce oxygen as a by-product. Some scientists are even exploring whether these bacteria could be put to use in mines or during **prolonged** space travel, where they could digest waste products and produce additional oxygen.

Other scientists wonder whether bacteria could be used to digest radioactive wastes. Scientists **introduced** one type of bacteria into water that contained dissolved uranium. The bacteria went to work, transforming the uranium-laden water into water mixed with a harmless solid. Geneticists—scientists who study genes—propose **customizing** bacteria to work on specific types of wastes, including nuclear wastes. Experiments have included inserting genes from one bacteria into another type of bacteria, creating a "superbug." Laboratory tests show that the superbug transforms toxic mercury in nuclear waste into less toxic forms of the substance.

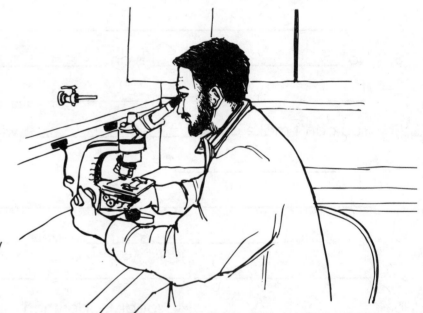

Use the passage on page 100 to circle the response that best defines each word as it is used in the passage. Use context clues and a dictionary if needed.

1.  common
    A.  multiple
    B.  ordinary
    C.  lower-class
    D.  poisonous

2.  waste
    A.  misuse
    B.  litter
    C.  unwanted by-products
    D.  leftovers

3.  strains
    A.  types
    B.  injuries
    C.  twists
    D.  pulls

4.  beneficial
    A.  cutting-edge
    B.  ordinary
    C.  advantageous
    D.  extraordinary

5.  toxic
    A.  playful
    B.  unscientific
    C.  uncorrupted
    D.  poisonous

6.  stimulates
    A.  excites to activity
    B.  changes
    C.  stirs
    D.  forces

7.  function
    A.  multiply
    B.  divide
    C.  work
    D.  care

8.  prolonged
    A.  extended
    B.  introductory
    C.  optimistic
    D.  enduring

9.  introduced
    A.  begun
    B.  exchange names
    C.  added
    D.  started

10.  customizing
    A.  mannered
    B.  tailoring
    C.  injecting
    D.  poisoning

Read the passage. Then, complete the activity on page 103.

# Survival

What would you do if you were **stranded** in the wilderness? You have probably read or heard about people who survive under seemingly impossible conditions. These people have been able to survive by focusing on three basic needs: water, food, and shelter.

Water is one of the few substances necessary to **sustain** life, but pure water may be difficult to find. Water can be **purified** by boiling it for three to five minutes. If there is a shortage of water, do not overexert yourself. Overexertion will cause you to **perspire** excessively, resulting in a salt deficiency that causes cramps, fatigue, and **dehydration**.

Feelings of hunger can be ignored with a positive attitude, but food is another necessity if you are lost or stranded for a longer period of time. Some people have to overcome their **aversion** to eating insects, earthworms, grasshoppers, and other animals that are easy to catch. Plants, however, should not be eaten unless they are identified as **edible**. Nuts are easy to identify and are nutritious. Knobby berries, such as blackberries and raspberries, are also simple to identify. You can also eat inner tree bark and the shoots of pine saplings. Pine needles can be simmered in hot water to produce a tea.

Protection from extreme temperatures is another concern. In heavy rains or snow, you can crawl under the snow or **vegetation** for shelter. A **makeshift** cave can be created by tunneling into the base of a thick evergreen tree, and using the tree **boughs** to line and insulate the cave. Clothing or other fabric can be used if you need to shield yourself from hot sun.

Remaining calm is extremely important in any emergency. Come up with a plan and don't waste time or energy by getting upset. Find a water source, identify food to gather, and find shelter. By focusing on these basics, you can turn yourself into a survivor.

Use the passage on page 102 to circle the response that best defines each word as it is used in the passage. Use context clues and a dictionary if needed.

1.  stranded

    A.  separated

    B.  upright

    C.  marooned

    D.  found

2.  sustain

    A.  extend

    B.  maintain

    C.  direct

    D.  hold

3.  purified

    A.  cleansed

    B.  baked

    C.  twisted

    D.  destroyed

4.  perspire

    A.  think

    B.  sweat

    C.  lunge

    D.  dehydrate

5.  dehydration

    A.  exhaustion

    B.  sickness

    C.  a severe reduction in body fluids

    D.  death

6.  aversion

    A.  attraction

    B.  repugnance

    C.  corruption

    D.  poisonous

7.  edible

    A.  fit to be eaten

    B.  easy to cook

    C.  corrected

    D.  harvested

8.  vegetation

    A.  animal life

    B.  roots

    C.  plant life

    D.  lazy

9.  makeshift

    A.  sturdy

    B.  timely

    C.  portable

    D.  temporary

10.  boughs

    A.  needles

    B.  branches

    C.  leaves

    D.  trunks

Read the passage. Then, write the metaphors and similes from the passage in the organizer.

# My Birthday

Our house was a beehive of activity. The whispering between my family members sounded like a swarm of bees. My heart beat like the flutter of a bird's wings. My birthday was only days away but it seemed like a ship off in the distance. Would it ever arrive? And when it did, what treasures would it carry?

On the day of my birthday, my mother got up early and started baking. The kitchen smelled like a bakery just before it opens its doors. The unfrosted cake was a giant drum that would lead the parade of things to come on my special day. Mother shooed me out of the kitchen before I could see how she would decorate the cake. Later I would see the snowdrifts of frosting arranged in mounds to represent a ski slope. My mother knew that skiing was one of my favorite hobbies.

Later that day, friends and family arrived like ants to a picnic. Each guest brought a gift and placed it on a leaning tower of presents not unlike the leaning Tower of Pisa. Each gift was beautifully wrapped, a welcome mat inviting me to open them to see what was inside.

My birthday was amazing. From dawn until dark the day was a celebration of me. I will remember my 14th birthday for a very long time.

| Metaphors | Similes |
|---|---|
|  |  |

Read the passage. Then, write the words from the word bank on the correct folder.

# File It Away

Fiona has a flair for filing. In fact, some say she is fastidious. Last Friday, Fiona's fuchsia-colored folders flew out of her filing cabinet and out the fifth-floor window. Fortunately for Fiona, her files survived the fall. But unfortunately, her files of words that begin with F got freakishly mixed up.

| | | | | |
|---|---|---|---|---|
| fallacy | feasible | fend | flair | fluster |
| forfeit | foreboding | formidable | fortify | foster |
| flourish | fictitious | famished | ferocious | foresight |
| fragment | fraudulent | frequency | fatigue | frugal |

Write the words from the word bank onto the correct folder.

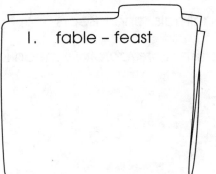

1.  fable – feast

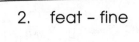

2.  feat – fine

3.  finery – foal

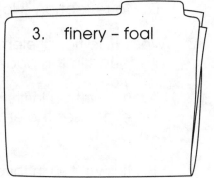

4.  fob – fort

5.  forte – frock

6.  frog – fuzz

Read the poem. Then, answer the questions.

# The Bee Is Not Afraid of Me

The bee is not afraid of me,
I know the butterfly.
The **pretty people in the woods**
Receive me cordially.

The brooks laugh louder when I come,
The breezes madder play.
Wherefore, mine eyes, thy silver mists?
Wherefore, O summer's day?

by Emily Dickinson

1. What is the purpose of this lyric poem?

   A. to express the poet's feelings about nature

   B. to show the habits of bees and butterflies

   C. to speak to the nature of death

   D. to reflect on a lost love

2. What traditional elements of a lyric are found in this poem?

   A. It is written in first person and expresses the emotions of the poet.

   B. It is written in third person and expresses the thoughts of the poet.

   C. It is written in third person and describes a series of actions.

   D. It is written in first person and tells of a true historical event.

3. What are the "pretty people in the woods"?

   A. neighbors who live in a house in the woods

   B. people camping in the woods

   C. fairies and elves

   D. birds, animals, and insects

4. What does the word *cordially* mean in this poem?

   A. politely

   B. with fear

   C. mockingly

   D. with joy

5. How does the author feel about her relationship with nature?

   _____

   _____

6. On a separate sheet of paper, write an essay comparing this poem with another poem written by Emily Dickinson. You can find her other poems in books or on the Internet.

Read the poem. Then, answer the questions.

# Ode to Autumn

Season of mists and mellow fruitfulness!
Close bosom-friend of the maturing sun;
Conspiring with him how to load and bless
With fruit the vines that round the thatch-eaves run;
To bend with apples the moss'd cottage-trees,
And fill all fruit with ripeness to the core;
To swell the gourd, and plump the hazel shells
With a sweet kernel; to set budding more,
And still more, later flowers for the bees,
Until they think warm days will never cease,
For Summer has o'er-brimmed **their clammy cells**.
by John Keats

1.  What makes this poem an ode?

    A.  It shows grief for something lost or dead.

    B.  It is a formal poem of praise for someone or something.

    C.  It tells the story of an actual historical event.

    D.  It has fourteen lines written in iambic pentameter.

2.  The excerpt above is only one stanza of the ode. The other stanzas probably contain

    A.  praise for autumn's plentiful harvest and weather.

    B.  a description of a death that took place during the fall of the year.

    C.  three lines each with five, seven, and five syllables.

    D.  complaints about autumn rain and frost.

3.  What does the poet refer to in the phrase "their clammy cells"?

    A.  the petals of a flower

    B.  the honey cells of a beehive

    C.  the prison cells in the local jail

    D.  the biological cells in a hazelnut

4.  List five things that you would praise about your favorite season.

    _____

    _____

    _____

    _____

    _____

5.  On a separate sheet of paper or on the computer, write a poem about your favorite season.

Read the poem. Then, answer the questions.

# The Eagle

He clasps the crag with crooked hands;
Close to the sea in lonely lands,
Ring'd with the **azure world**, he stands.

The wrinkled sea beneath him crawls;
He watches from his mountain walls,
And like a thunderbolt, he falls.

by Alfred, Lord Tennyson

1. What is the poem about?

   _____

   _____

2. What simile appears in this poem?

   _____

3. What does the poet mean by "the azure world"?

   _____

4. Would you classify this poem as a ballad, an elegy, or a lyric poem? Give a reason for your choice.

   _____

   _____

5. What is the rhyme scheme of this poem?

   _____

Read the poem. Then, answer the questions.

# Ozymandias

I met a traveller from an antique land
Who said: Two vast and trunkless legs of stone
Stand in the desert...Near them, on the sand,
Half sunk, a shattered visage lies, whose frown,
And wrinkled lip, and sneer of cold command,
Tell that its sculptor well those passions read
Which yet survive, stamped on these lifeless things,
The hand that mocked them, and the heart that fed:
And on the pedestal these words appear:
"My name is Ozymandias, king of kings:
Look on my works, ye Mighty, and despair!"
Nothing beside remains. Round the decay
Of that colossal wreck, boundless and bare
The lone and level sands stretch far away.
by Percy Bysshe Shelley

1. What is the main idea of this poem?

   A. The pyramids were once part of larger statues.

   B. All kings and kingdoms eventually fall.

   C. Egypt is a fascinating place to visit.

   D. Archaeologists can learn from the past.

2. What is the irony in the poem "Ozymandias"?

   A. The sculpture of the great king had fallen apart.

   B. The person telling the story was awed by the great works of Ozymandias.

   C. The pedestal inscription indicates a great kingdom, but there is nothing left but desert.

   D. The legs of stone belonged to a king killed by his subjects.

3. What is the best description of the statue?

   A. Two legs are still standing. The head of the sculpture is half buried in the sand.

   B. The head of the sculpture is on the pedestal, and two legs are lying nearby.

   C. The head of the sculpture and a stone heart are lying by a pedestal.

   D. The body of the statue is still whole, but the legs are missing.

4. Describe the face of the statue.

   _____

   _____

   _____

Read the poem. Then, answer the questions on page 111.

# Dick Turpin's Ride

"Dick Turpin, bold Dick, hie away," was the cry
Of my pals, who were startled, you guess.
The pistols were leveled, the bullets whizzed by,
As I jumped on the back of Black Bess.

Three officers, mounted, led forward the chase,
Resolved in the capture to share;
But I smiled on their efforts, though swift was their pace,
As I urged on my bonny black mare.

"Hark away, hark away!" Still onward we press,
And I saw by the glimmers of morn,
Full many a mile on the back of Black Bess
That night I was gallantly borne.

When the spires of York Minister now burst on my view,
And the chimes they are ringing a knell—
"Halt, halt! my brave mare, they no longer pursue."
As she halted, she staggered, she fell.

Her breathings are over, all hushed to her grave,
My poor Black Bess, once my pride.
But her heart she had burst, her rider to save—
For Dick Turpin she lived and she died.

Anonymous 19th century poem

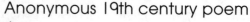

Use the poem on page 110 to answer the questions.

1. What is this poem about?

   A. A man is captured and killed.

   B. A man rides his horse to escape arrest.

   C. Officers ride their horses to death.

   D. A pursuit by officers leads to an arrest.

2. What detail of the poem foreshadows a death?

   A. the friends calling out warnings to Dick Turpin

   B. the glimmer of morning on the horizon

   C. the bells ringing a knell, which is done for funerals

   D. the horse's breathing coming to an end

3. What is York Minister?

   A. a graveyard

   B. a boat

   C. a farm

   D. a church

4. Dick Turpin was a real-life highwayman, a robber of stagecoaches. How can you tell in the poem that he is a criminal?

   A. He rides a fast horse.

   B. He rides his horse to death.

   C. He is being chased by officers.

   D. His friends are shooting at him.

5. How did Dick Turpin feel about his horse?

   A. He didn't care about her, even when she died.

   B. He loved her and admired the sacrifice she made for him.

   C. He was proud of how fast she could run.

   D. He had no particular feelings for her.

6. If this poem had been about Dick Turpin's arrest, what event might foreshadow that?

   A. Dick Turpin shoots and kills one of the officers chasing him.

   B. Dick Turpin falls off his horse and the officers catch up to him.

   C. Three officers resolve in the capture Dick Turpine.

   D. Dick Turpin thinks back to a time when he was arrested.

Read the tale. Then, complete the activities on page 113.

# The Intruder

"Come in, officer, thanks for coming," Mr. Baird said as he opened the door and invited the officer in. "As I told the 911 operator, we got back from our nightly walk and noticed that our house had been broken into."

"Slow down and tell me exactly what happened," the officer said calmly as he took out a pad of paper and a pen to take some notes.

Mr. Baird began slowly to retell the events of the evening, "Well, my wife made us some of her delicious stew for dinner, but it was too hot to eat, so we decided to go for a walk and let the stew cool down a bit. When we returned, I immediately knew something was up and said to the others, "Somebody has been eating my stew."

"And that's when I noticed that someone had been eating some of my stew, too," Mrs. Baird added in.

"Yeah, and then I looked at my bowl of stew and said, 'Somebody has being eating my stew, and has eaten it all gone!'" explained Bailey Baird as he showed the officer the empty bowl.

"Boy that kid has a squeaky voice," the officer thought to himself but then responded aloud, "Calm down, son. Go on."

"Then we went into the living room where I knew immediately that someone had been sitting my favorite recliner," Mr. Baird explained.

"And I noticed someone had been sitting in my chair, too," added Mrs. Baird.

"Yeah, and then I noticed that somebody had been sitting in my chair and had broken it," wailed Bailey Baird showing the officer.

"That screechy voice is going to make me lose it," the officer thought smiling and nodding with feigned interest. "So did the intruder go anywhere else in the house?" inquired the officer.

"Well, after we saw the living room, we dialed 911 immediately," Mr. Baird explained. "Let's go take a look," he said leading the officer to the rooms down the hall. "We're redoing the boy's room—new paint and carpet—so we moved his bed into our room so he wouldn't have to inhale the paint fumes," Mr. Baird continued as he opened the door to the master bedroom. "Well, I'll be," Mr. Baird growled, "Somebody has been sleeping in my bed!"

"And somebody has been sleeping in my bed, too" added Mrs. Baird as she noticed the crumpled up comforter on her bed."

"And somebody has been sleeping in my bed too and she is still there!" Bailey Baird screeched even more loudly than before.

Just then a young blonde girl woke up startled and popped out of the small bed like a jack-in-a-box, and ran down the steps.

The officer radioed for back-up. "Do you want to press charges, Mr. Baird?" asked the officer.

"Of course I want to press charges! That's illegal entry. These two-legged humans think they own the place, don't they?"

Use the tale on page 112 to complete the activities.

1.  What folktale is this a retelling of?

    _____

2.  Draw a Venn diagram to compare and contrast this telling of the tale to another version you have heard or read.

3.  On a separate sheet of paper or on the computer, write another version of this folktale or another folktale that you know. Change the setting, the point of view, or the characters of your tale.

Read the tale. Then, complete the activities on page 115.

# It's True!

My great-uncle, Ole Bergstrom, was the greatest **logger** ever to log in the young nation of the United States. No one could beat him! Uncle Ole came to this great nation from Finland in 1860 for the farmland promised in those Old World posters. Uncle Ole brought with him my great-aunt, Trina. On the voyage from the old country, they ran into a terrible storm at sea. The ship's crew couldn't get the engines working hot enough to make any headway. Well, my Uncle Ole stormed down to the ship's boiler and loaded it with coal faster than the whole crew combined knocking three men out silly in his hurry. The ship was freed from the storm's grip and managed to arrive safely in the New York Harbor.

New York City could have had its hold on Uncle Ole, but instead he and Trina headed toward the great forests of the northwest—a logger's paradise. Westward they traveled by rail, by stagecoach, by **steamer**, and by foot until they reached the Michigan North Woods. I heard tell that when the train derailed in Albany, Uncle Ole lifted it back on the tracks all while he was suffering a touch of fever he caught after carrying a lame horse 20 miles just east of that city.

When Uncle Ole reached his **claim**, he wasted no time building a house. He pulled up four beech trees, braided their trunks into four walls that made a cozy little home. I heard it said that one stomp of his foot would clear an acre of trees. But when the call came for loggers, Uncle Ole left his cozy home and his wife and hired himself to Mr. Amos Macomb for the winter. Macomb's logging company hired over 100 workers—**drivers**, **sawyers**, cooks, haulers, foremen, stable boys, and Uncle Ole who could do it all.

Stories are told about the day Oscar Dobbers' ox went lame and Ole pulled the load to give the beast a week's rest and when a **felling** crew got lost in a blizzard, Ole not only found them, he built them a snow house and for four days warmed them with his stories until the storm blew out. Then there was the time when the Au Sable River suffered its worst **logjam**; it was Uncle Ole who devised the solution. He ordered all the company's men to melt snow by rolling back and forth in it to raise the river level. Uncle Ole grabbed a **peavey**, pounced on the logjam, and single-handedly scattered those huge logs. Loggers for miles away said that the thuds and roars and cracks and screeches sounded as if heaven's giants were bowling. Uncle Ole **chortled** and laughed until all logs were again on their way downstream and the drivers could again guide the load to market. But the last we heard tell of Uncle Ole, drivers say he rode the lead logs downstream like George Washington crossing the Delaware and disappeared around the river bend and was never seen again.

And Trina, she kept mum.

Use the tale on page 114 to complete the activities.

1. Place a **T** by each event that could be true and an **E** by each event that is an exaggeration.

   _____ Uncle Ole came to the United State from Finland.

   _____ He loaded the coal into the ship's boiler.

   _____ He lifted a derailed train and placed it back on its tracks.

   _____ He built a house out of beech trees.

   _____ One stomp of his foot could clear an acre of trees.

   _____ He carried the load pulled by an ox for a week.

   _____ He rescued a felling crew and built them a snow house.

   _____ He broke up a logjam with his bare hands.

   _____ He rode logs of the logjam down the river.

2. Write the definition of each word as used in this tale. Use context clues and a dictionary if needed.

   logger: _____

   claim: _____

   steamer: _____

   drivers: _____

   sawyers: _____

   felling: _____

   logjam: _____

   peavey: _____

   chortled: _____

3. Read another American tall tale from a book or the Internet. On a separate sheet of paper or on the computer, write an American tall tale. Be sure to include a setting of settling the western part of the United States and lots of exaggeration.

Read the tale. Then, complete the activities on page 117.

# Fee, Fi!

It isn't a lot of fun to be so big. The other folks poke fun of me and snicker and call me a monster. Some days they are just downright mean. That's why me and the missus decided to go and live in the wilderness by ourselves. We moved up into them hills, high overlookin' our village in the valley. The only way to reach our new home was to climb a grapevine rope. We didn't take much—just our chickens, my harp, and the money we had saved.

I keep us fed by farmin' a wee patch of wheat and barley, by tamin' a herd of wild goats that lived on the hill before we got there. My wife cared for the house and the chickens. She made the bread and fixed the food I provided.

One day a young, yellow-haired kid came up from the village. My wife was delighted to have some company, especially a young'n, and she fed him and showed him around the place. That little rascal repaid my wife's kindness by stealin' one of our chickens—a setting hen. I swore I'd teach him a thing or two if he were to ever step foot on our property again.

Believe it or not, that boy did come back and this time he took the money we had saved. Neither me nor my wife did see him come, but we saw him go. My wife chased him wavin' her broom and shoutin', "Fee, fi, I smell a rat! Be off with you, you bony brat."

We thought that was the last we'd see of that kid, but a few months later he came back. I was out in the garden when he came sneakin' into kitchen. When my wife's back was turned, he crouched under the table just waitin' for an opportunity to steal my harp. When I came in, I smelled that funny smell of the village and said, "Fee, Fi, no joy! I smell a little boy." Out from under the table the little kid did jump up like a Jack-in-the-box and reached over and snatched my harp! Me and my wife, we ran after that little scamp, but just as I was about to grab him, he reach the vine and sailed down it. Well, I chased after the boy down the vine, but when he got to the village, he yelled that I was tryin' to kill him. So the townspeople came to his defense with their axes, pitchforks, and clubs.

I yelled, "I ain't tryin' to kill him. That boy stole from me and my wife. He took my chicken, my money, and my harp."

But the folks weren't much in the mood for discussin' things civilized. So I ran back to the vine as quick as my giant legs would carry me promisin' to leave that dreadful village forever. I pulled up the vine and was never to enter the village again or hear from the villagers again—at least until they got word of my hen who started layin' golden eggs, but that's a story for another time.

Use the tale on page 116 to complete the activities.

1. Place the following events in order **1–7** as they occurred in the story

   _____ The boy steals the harp.

   _____ The giant and his wife move up into the hills.

   _____ The boy steals a chicken.

   _____ The boy steals the money.

   _____ The villagers came after the giant with axes, pitchforks, and clubs.

   _____ The villagers teased the giant.

   _____ The wife fed the boy and showed him around the place.

2. Label the emotion expressed in each of these sentences.

   *It isn't a lot of fun to be so big.* _____

   *I keep us fed by farmin' a wee patch of wheat and barley.* _____

   *That boy did come back!* _____

   *My wife chased him wavin' her broom and shoutin'.* _____

   *So the townspeople came to his defense with their axes, pitchforks, and clubs.*

   _____

3. Folktales often use improper grammar and spelling to enhance the setting of the story. Circle the grammatical and spelling errors in the tale. (Hint: There are 18.)

4. What common folktale does this tale remind you of? (Look in a book of folktales or on the Internet if it is not familiar to you.)

   _____

5. How is this version of the folktale different from the common version?

   _____

   _____

6. On a separate sheet of paper or on the computer, write your version of the next chapter of this folktale from the giant's perspective.

Read the passage. Then, complete page 119.

# Drive Like Jehu

When I was young, my mother told me a story about an old king named Jehu.

Jehu was this guy who drove his chariot like he was in the Indy 500. No one could keep up with him and he was crazy enough that no one even tried. He also had a good eye for shooting his bow, but, his chariot driving was something else!

You might ask yourself why I am telling you a story learned in my youth. Truth is, the story of Jehu is not unlike a story about my dad. You see, my dad drives fast—too fast my mom says—but my dad just says he likes being **punctual**.

To get to our school, my sister and I get a mile ride to our bus stop. That's all the closer the school bus could come. Usually my sister and I squashed ourselves into the cab of Dad's pickup—rain or shine, snow or ice, winter, spring, and autumn.

One week last autumn we had a **torrential** storm which caused roads to close all over the district and knocked the power out for days. Schools were closed for four days which was great—until you think about the fact that we'll be making up those days in the hot days of June. Anyway, the first day back to school after the storm presented the setting to my story.

We started our **clip** to the bus stop as usual with Dad flooring the pedal once he got to the main road. Now **unbeknownst** to us, the rain had destroyed the road ahead creating a **crevice** about 10 feet (about 3m) wide and 4–8 feet (1–2.5m) deep. **Barreling** toward this unknown canyon, my dad drove faster and faster.

"You drive like Jehu," I muttered under my breath.

By the time we saw the **gully's** gap, we were maybe two stone throws away. Quick as a wink, Dad figured he had two choices—either he could slam on the brakes and probably skid us into the chasm, or he could speed up and try jumping the hole. Dad made up his mind and jammed that pedal all the way to the floor, our heads whipped back in response, and we rocketed closer and closer to the **void**. Dad's tongue peeked out as he concentrated on his mission. The pickup truck screamed, the wind whistled into the less-than-tightly-sealed windows. When we got to the **brink** of the **cavity**, I closed my eyes. I remember the sensation, that moment of suspension, floating, and then the jolting bump as we landed safely on the other side.

Without a spoken word, Dad slowed down and we eased to the bus stop. The bus arrived two minutes later. The rest of the day was a **haze**; I couldn't talk about the ride to anybody. Maybe it was just too much like a dream.

Use the passage on page 118 to complete the activities.

1.  Describe the setting of the story.

    _____

    _____

2.  How does the author draw from the story his mother told him to make his story more interesting?

    _____

    _____

    _____

3.  Write the definition of each word as used in this tale. Use context clues and a dictionary if needed.

    punctual: _____

    torrential: _____

    clip: _____

    unbeknownst: _____

    crevice: _____

    barreling: _____

    gully: _____

    void: _____

    brink: _____

    cavity: _____

    haze: _____

4.  On a separate sheet of paper or on the computer, write a personal narrative. Use a legend or religious story to enhance the telling of your narrative.

Read the passage. Then, compete the activities on page 121.

# They Can't Help It

The bell rings for the next period. "You forgot to give us homework!" a student in the front row cries.

That's probably a firstborn asking for homework. Researcher Frank J. Sulloway found most firstborns respectful of authority. They can be pretty bossy and authoritarian themselves, but only because they want to keep things running smoothly. They can be reformers, too. They often lead fashionable or socially acceptable reforms. For example, many firstborn baby boomers led movements that cracked down on drugs and cigarette smoking.

Laterborns have to compete for parental attention. That's not bad, Sulloway claims. Laterborns learn tolerance and openness to new ideas. They often begin new movements in science and politics and do not worry whether they are socially acceptable movements. For example, laterborns helped start the French Revolution.

Middleborns play an important role in science and politics, too, according to Sulloway. They ease cooperation between groups.

When family size decreases, a higher proportion of children are firstborns. Fewer children are middleborns. Family size decreased in the Depression of the 1930s and that generation grew up to defend and accept authority.

You probably know firstborns who challenge authority, middleborns who never cooperate, and laterborns who follow rules. Galileo and Einstein, two firstborns, developed bold, creative ideas about science. Exceptions exist, but other studies confirm that birth order influences behavior. So, all of you laterborns, please excuse the rule-following, authority-loving firstborns asking for more homework. Ask the middleborns to referee if anyone gets too upset about it.

Use the passage on page 120 to complete the activities.

1. Are you a firstborn, middleborn, or laterborn? Using the passage as a guide, write a generalization about people who share your birth order.

_____

_____

2. How do you differ from that generalization?

_____

Read the following generalizations about birth order. Based on the information you read in the passage, write **V** for valid or **I** for invalid.

3. _____ Most firstborns follow rules.

4. _____ Laterborns are always more tolerant than firstborns.

5. _____ Middleborns tend to be more cooperative than firstborns.

6. _____ Firstborns never start new political movements.

7. _____ When family size decreases, the new generation has fewer middleborns.

Read the generalizations. Decide which group of people or events are being described. Then, complete the sentence.

8. Many lead political movements to preserve the status quo. This generalization applies to _____ .

9. They proposed some of the world's most radical ideas in science or politics. This generalization applies to _____ .

10. They often relate well to adults because they tend to respect authority figures. This generalization applies to _____ .

# Answer Key

**Page 5**

Check students' citations. I. The grooming behavior of birds is a behavior that helps them to stay alive. 2. Answers will vary but should include evidence from the text.

**Page 7**

I. B; 2. C; 3. A; 4. Answers will vary but should include evidence from the text.
5. Answers will vary.

**Page 9**

Answers in the graphic organizer will vary but should include evidence from the text.

**Page 11**

I. D; 2. C; 3. D; 4. D; 5. A; 6. B; 7. by paragraphs with subtitles; 8. Answers will vary but should include evidence from the text.

**Page 13**

I. This article presents a view of Mozart's life. 2–3. Answers will vary but should include evidence from the text. 4. compose: write music; prodigy: a talented child; keyboard: keys on a piano; concert: a public performance of music; composition: a piece of written music; opera: a show in which the actors sing; symphony: a long piece of music; commission: an amount paid for a service; overture: a piece of music played at the beginning of an opera or play

**Page 15**

I. D; 2. B or A; 3. G; 4. E; 5. D; 6. J; 7. B; 8. D; 9. F; 10. H; 11. H; 12. G or H; 13. C; 14. E; 15. F

**Page 17**

I. Who: Three Students; What: represented their school at the International Exhibit of Student Art; When: June 17–21; Where: Paris, France; Why: Answers will vary but should include evidence from the text. 2. Answers will vary. 3. Answers will vary but possible answers include on the Internet. 4. Answers will vary.

**Page 19**

I. A. I. thought lights were omen;
I. A. 2. thought lights were omen of war;
I. B. Europeans; I. B. 2. thought lights were an omen of the end of time;
II. A. I. solar-powered; III. B. cause atmospheric disturbances;
III. B. 2. communication systems disrupted;
III. B. 4. satellite computers malfunction;
IV. A. light up pink, red, green, and blue;
IV. B. colorless waves

**Page 21**

Derek Chu lives at 125 and plays hockey. Lily Lee lives at 116 and plays lacrosse. Gabe Park lives at 118 and likes doing bike tricks. Luke Katz lives at 132 and likes to skateboard.

**Page 22**

Venn diagram should have Rachel in the middle section; Nadia and Jaime in the section intersecting math and band; Mario in math only section; Nicole and Hannah in English only section; Lee, Ian, and Ryan in the band only section.

**Page 23**

I. A Serendipitous Find; 2. A Mythical Visitor; 3. Instincts Save a Life; 4. Shock at Lack of Respect

**Page 25**

I. Mummies reveal a lot about the person who was mummified. 2. C; 3–4. Answers will vary but should include evidence from the text.

# Answer Key

## Page 27
1–3. Answers will vary but should include evidence from the text. 4. Answers will vary.

## Page 29
1. Answers will vary. 2. Answers will vary but should include evidence from the text. 3. Answers will vary. 4. Order of events: 4, 3, 1, 2, 5, 7, 6

## Page 31
1. A. male; B. mostly male; 2. A. pale, staring eyes; B. spasms, frothing at mouth; 3. A. bite others, sleep during day; B. bite others, irritability; 4. A. can rise up after death, difficult to kill; B. look lifelike after death

## Page 33
1. Prairie dogs are members of the squirrel family. They look different. Some breeds of prairie dogs are threatened or endangered. 2. Prairie dogs live underground. They have a sophisticated form of communication. 3. They are a community that looks out for each other. 4. remote: far away; bustling: busy; intricate: detailed; descendants: those with relatives from the past; fringes: outer edges; intruders: unwanted visitors

## Page 35
1–3. Answers will vary but should include evidence from the text. 4. Answers will vary.

## Page 37
1. Order of events: 2, 7, 4, 1, 5, 8, 6, 3; 2. He had heard that dogs take on the characteristics and looks of their owners. 3. spot: predicament; persuasive: able to persuade; rebuttal: argument; invigorating: energizing; 4. in a pickle: in a difficult situation; to a tee: to perfection; tongue-tied: unable to talk

## Page 39
1. Order of events: 3, 10, 5, 1, 4, 8, 2, 9, 5, 7; 2. ominous: suggesting something bad is going to happen; boding: omen; stifling: making it difficult to breathe; flinch: to pull back quickly; gale: a strong wind; precipitation: rain; 3. Answers will vary.

## Page 41
1. Order of events: 3, 10, 7, 2, 12, 5, 1, 8, 6, 11, 4, 9; 2 A. Problem: The boys needed new pajamas. B. Rising Action: The family went to Grandma and Grandpa's house. C. Turning Point: They opened their presents but there weren't any pajamas. D. Falling Action: Mom found out about the ripped pajamas. E. Resolution: Mom took the boys to the store to buy their own pajamas.

## Page 43
1. E; 2. C; 3. C; 4. E; 5. C; 6. E; 7. E; 8. C; 9. C; 10. E; 11. Answers will vary. 12. Answers will vary but may include that the family sleds down hills in their neighborhood.

## Page 45
1. O'Meara was concerned that the Munsee Delaware language would die out. 2. O'Meara made recordings and wrote a dictionary to help preserve the language. 3. Dutch settlers; 4. His suggestion was ignored. 5. Ninety Delaware were massacred.

## Page 47
1. F; 2. O; 3. F; 4. O; 5. O; 6. F; 7. O; 8. O; 9. F; 10. Answers will vary.

## Page 49
1. F; 2. O; 3. O; 4. F; 5. F; 6. F; 7. O; 8. F; 9. Answers will vary.

# Answer Key

## Page 51
1. C; 2. devious; exiled; drum up; used her charm; treacherous; 3. to imply that she was improper, a risk-taker, or both; 4–5. Answers will vary but should include evidence from the text.

## Page 53
1. B; 2–3. Answers will vary but should include evidence from the text. 4. Answers will vary.

## Page 55
1. C; 2. C; 3. Answers will vary but may include that the author uses questions to draw the reader in. 4. There would be more details and more technical terms. There might be some research evidence. 5. leave or get out of the way; 6. Answers will vary.

## Page 57
1–4. Answers will vary but should include evidence from the text.

## Page 59
Check students' citations. 1. The clouds gathering in the sky or the title. 2. She didn't want to leave Zack out in the storm. 3. Answers will vary but should include evidence from the text. 4. when the sound of the storm grew distant; 5. a tornado

## Page 61
Check students' citations. 1. Answers will vary but may include that Katie does not like the way her sister acts and that her mother likes Grace better. 2. that she is vengeful and jealous; 3. that Grace takes advantage of Katie; 4. that sometimes she is not respectful of Katie and her things; 5. that they do not get along well; 6. that the mother may be worried more about Grace since she lives at college; 7. Answers will vary.

## Page 63
Check students' citations. 1. third person; 2. omniscient; the reader "hears" both characters' thoughts; 3. Mark tells himself to keep his hand from shaking. 4. Mark might not have enough money to pay for the card. 5. Answers will vary but should include evidence from the text. 6. Answers will vary but should include evidence from the text. 7. You would not know the value of the card or the difficulty of Mark's decision. You would also not know how much the seller of the card needed the money or why.

## Page 65
Check students' citations. 1. D; 2. Bill thinks playing with Avery is not a challenge, indicated in Bill's conversation with his mom. 3. Bill realizes Avery is growing up and becoming more of a challenge, indicated in Bill's conversation with Avery at the end of the story. 4. Avery is excited about playing with Bill and wants to show him that he can be a challenge, indicated in the narration: "He was excited." 5. Answers will vary but should include evidence from the text.

## Page 67
Check students' citations. 1. The author is trying to convince the reader that allowing the use oxygen canisters when climbing Mount Everest is a bad practice. 2. Answers will vary but may include that it encourages climbers to go beyond their natural instincts. 3. Answers will vary but should include evidence from the text. 4. opinion-based; 5. Answers will vary but should include evidence from the text. 6. *The great mountain has dared many a thrill-seeker to scale its fortress. Are used oxygen canisters and corpses of paying clients fitting ornaments for such a goddess to wear?*

# Answer Key

## Page 68
1. K; 2. A; 3. E; 4. L; 5. G; 6. D; 7. H; 8. I; 9. B; 10. F; 11. J; 12. C

## Page 69
1. D; 2. C; 3. G; 4. I; 5. B; 6. F; 7. A; 8. E; 9. Answers will vary.

## Page 71
Check students' citations. 1. Answers will vary but may include compassionate, hardworking, and responsible. 2. the economic hardships; 3. Answers will vary. 4. He sees beggars asking for leftovers. 5. Answers will vary.

## Page 73
Answers will vary but should include evidence from the text.

## Page 75
1–2. Answers will vary. 3. Answers will vary but should include evidence from the text. 4. Answers will vary.

## Page 77
Check students' citations. 1–4. Answers will vary but should include evidence from the text. 5. Answers will vary.

## Page 79
1. small, brown, grass-roofed huts; sight; 2. steep, snow-capped; sight; 3. cold; touch; 4. barking, braying; hearing; 5. heavy, woolen; touch; 6. spicy; smell or taste; 7. distant, terraced; sight; 8. strong, bitter; smell; 9. distant cries; hearing; 10. red-gold embers; sight; 11. Answers will vary.

## Page 81
1. Answers will vary but should include evidence from the text. 2. extensive: large; ornamented: decorated; disposed: set; obscured: hidden; wafted: to move lightly;

shad: fish; 3. Answers will vary.

## Page 83
1. Location: campsite; Time of Day: night; Time of the Year: probably summer; Real or imaginary: imaginary; 2. The conflict in the story is that Tristan is missing. 3. Answers will vary but should include evidence from the story. 4. The characters in the story are Keisha, Arianna, Quiana, and Tristan. 5. Answers will vary but should include evidence from the story. 6. Answers will vary.

## Page 85
1. The setting take place at home, in the car, and at the bowling alley. 2–3. Answers will vary but should include evidence from the text. 4. Answers will vary.

## Page 87
1. a middle school; 2. Principal Rivera, Matt, and Mason; Descriptions will vary. 3. A car in the visitors' parking lot was keyed. 4. Matt and Mason tell Mr. Rivera what they saw. 5. The turning point is when Mr. Rivera confronts Matt. 6. mystery; 7. Matt immediately was defensive and he admits to leaving his classroom. 8. Answers will vary.

## Page 89
1. C; 2. A; 3. B; 4. A; 5. B; 6. A

## Page 91
Check students' citations. 1. Demetri, Sean, Demetri's mother, Mrs. Foster; Descriptions will vary. 2. Demetri's garage; other neighborhood places; school; 3. The boys need a new computer chip but don't have enough money to buy one. 4. making money by cleaning, washing cars, babysitting; 5. Mrs. Foster gives them a computer-store coupon. 6. The boys buy the chip they need and took the robot to the science fair.

# Answer Key

## Page 93

1. Mr. Mifflin, Mrs. Mifflin, Titania, and Bock; Answers will vary but should include evidence from the text. 2. the bookshop; 3. The owner of the bookstore thinks Titania is spoiled. 4. Titania tries to impress her new employer and gives Mrs. Mifflin flowers. 5. Mrs. Mifflin is captivated by Titania's gift and shows her around the store. 6. Titania gives the dog a bone. 7. Titania gives presents to the owner's wife and dog. She is very polite and sweet, contrary to Mr. Mifflin's preconceived notion.

## Page 94

1. C; 2. D; 3. F; 4. H; 5. G; 6. A; 7. E; 8. B; 9. I; 10. J

## Page 95

Check students' illustrations. 1. time passes quickly; 2. listening closely; 3. got it exactly right; 4. Answers will vary.

## Page 96

1. Henry Ford; Answer will vary. 2. linen; Answer will vary. 3. Miami; Answer will vary. 4. email; Answer will vary. 5. pyramid; Answer will vary. 6. historical fiction; Answer will vary. 7. bottle; Answer will vary. 8. Atlantic Ocean; Answer will vary. 9. rock and roll; Answer will vary. 10. Elvis; Answer will vary. 11. novel; Answer will vary. 12. yard; Answer will vary.

## Page 97

1. contorted; 2. congested; 3. conjured; 4. prostrate; 5. protesters; 6. conduct; 7. proximate, 8. procrastinated; 9. proclaimed; 10. consulted; 11. concluded; 12. converged; 13. provoking

## Page 98

1. A; 2. C; 3. O; 4. F; 5. F; 6. I; 7. N; Answer to the riddle: a coffin.

## Page 99

1. pen; sword; words are more powerful than weapons; 2. do; Romans; behave to fit in; 3. man; island; people need each other; 4. omelet; eggs; sometimes you have to break things to make other things; 5. pot; boils; when you're anxiously watching something, it seem like it takes longer; 6. actions; words; what you do is more important than what you say; 7. cooks; broth; sometimes too many people involved leads to trouble; 8. bite; hand; be kind to those who are kind to you.

## Page 101

1. B; 2. C; 3. A; 4. C; 5. D; 6. A; 7. C; 8. A; 9. C; 10. B

## Page 103

1. C; 2. B; 3. A; 4. B; 5. C; 6. B; 7. A; 8. C; 9. D; 10. B

## Page 104

Metaphors: house was a beehive of activity; unfrosted cake was a giant drum that would lead the parade of things to come; each gift was beautifully wrapped, a welcome mat inviting me to open them to see what was inside; Similes: whispering sounded like a swarm of bees; my heart beat like the flutter of a bird's wings; my birthday seemed like a ship off in the distance; kitchen smelled like a bakery; family arrived like ants at a picnic

# Answer Key

## Page 105

1. fallacy, feasible, famished, fatigue; 2. fend, fictitious, ferocious; 3. flair, fluster, flourish, foresight; 4. forfeit, foreboding, formidable; 5. fortify, foster, fragment, fraudulent, frequency; 6. frugal

## Page 106

1. A; 2. A; 3. D; 4. A; 5. Answers will vary but may include that she feels welcomed by her friends in nature. 6. Answers will vary.

## Page 107

1. B; 2. A; 3. B; 4. Answers will vary. 5. Answers will vary.

## Page 108

1. Answers will vary but should include evidence from the text. 2. like a thunderbolt, he falls; 3. the sky; 4. a lyric poem because it is musical and expresses an image from nature; 5. *aaa/bbb*

## Page 109

1. B; 2. C; 3. A; 4. The expression on the face is cold and sneering.

## Page 111

1. B; 2. C; 3. D; 4. C; 5. B; 6. C

## Page 113

1. Goldilocks and the Three Bears; 2. Answers will vary but should include evidence from the text. 3. Answers will vary.

## Page 115

1. T, T, E, T, E, E, T, E, E; 2. logger: lumberjack; claim: a piece of land that one owns; steamer: large boat; drivers: people who move the logs down the river; sawyers: people who saw logs; felling: cutting down; logjam: where logs come together and stop the river from flowing; peavey: a large hook; chortled: laughed; 3. Answers will vary.

## Page 117

1. Order of events: 6, 2, 4, 5, 7, 1, 3; 2. sadness, pride, anger, anger, fear; 3. Circled, in order of occurrence: me and the missus; them; overlookin', farmin', tamin', young'n, stealin', me nor my wife; wavin', shoutin', sneakin' waitin', tryin', ain't tryin', me and my wife, discussin', promisin', layin'; 4. Jack and the Beanstalk; 5–6. Answers will vary.

## Page 119

1. Answers will vary but may include a road destroyed by a flood. 2. The author has the character compare his father to a character from a story he heard. 3. punctual: on time; torrential: heavy rain; clip: fast pace; unbeknownst: unknown; crevice: a large crack in the earth; barreling: moving quickly; gully: a small ditch or ravine; void: empty; brink: edge; cavity: a hole in the earth; haze: unclear; 4. Answers will vary.

## Page 121

1. Answers will vary but should include evidence from the text. 2. Answers will vary. 3. V; 4. I; 5. V; 6. I; 7. V; 8. firstborns; 9. laterborns; 10. firstborns

# Notes